About Island Press

Since 1984, the nonprofit organization Island Press has been stimulating, shaping, and communicating ideas that are essential for solving environmental problems worldwide. With more than 1,000 titles in print and some 30 new releases each year, we are the nation's leading publisher on environmental issues. We identify innovative thinkers and emerging trends in the environmental field. We work with world-renowned experts and authors to develop cross-disciplinary solutions to environmental challenges.

Island Press designs and executes educational campaigns, in conjunction with our authors, to communicate their critical messages in print, in person, and online using the latest technologies, innovative programs, and the media. Our goal is to reach targeted audiences—scientists, policy makers, environmental advocates, urban planners, the media, and concerned citizens—with information that can be used to create the framework for long-term ecological health and human well-being.

Island Press gratefully acknowledges major support from The Bobolink Foundation, Caldera Foundation, The Curtis and Edith Munson Foundation, The Forrest C. and Frances H. Lattner Foundation, The JPB Foundation, The Kresge Foundation, The Summit Charitable Foundation, Inc., and many other generous organizations and individuals.

The opinions expressed in this book are those of the author(s) and do not necessarily reflect the views of our supporters.

Building for People

Building for People

Designing Livable,
Affordable,
Low-Carbon Communities

Michael Eliason, AIA

ISLANDPRESS | Washington | Covelo

© 2024 Michael Eliason

All rights reserved under International and Pan-American Copyright Conventions. No part of this book may be reproduced in any form or by any means without permission in writing from the publisher: Island Press, 2000 M Street, NW, Suite 480-B, Washington, DC 20036-3319.

Library of Congress Control Number: 2024935668

All Island Press books are printed on environmentally responsible materials.

Manufactured in the United States of America
10 9 8 7 6 5 4 3 2 1

Keywords: Affordable housing, air pollution, Baugruppe, building code, child-friendly district, climate change, community participation, decarbonization, design competition, ecodistrict, economic diversity, extreme heat, fossil-fuel-free district, German development models, green space, housing, land use planning, mass timber, micro unit, mobility, net zero, noise pollution, open building, Passive House, planning regulations, point access block, productive district, public health, public space, single-stair building, social mixing, sponge city, Transit Oriented Development (TOD), urban policy, water loop, zoning

Contents

Foreword: Urbanism in the Planetary Crisis by Alex Steffen   *ix*
Preface   *xiii*
Acknowledgments   *xv*
Introduction   *xvii*

Chapter 1: The Compact, Climate Adaptive Ecodistrict   1

Chapter 2: Rethinking Urban Development in the United States   13

Part I: Planning the Ecodistrict   21

Chapter 3: The Productive District   23

Chapter 4: Net Zero and Fossil-Fuel-Free Districts   31

Chapter 5: Unlocking Ecodistricts with Better Regulations   37

Chapter 6: Planning the Ecodistrict   47

Chapter 7: Community Participation   57

Part II: Quality of Life and Public Health   65

Chapter 8: Mobility and the District of Short Distances   67

Chapter 9: A Good Economic and Social Mix   79

Chapter 10: Urban Places and Spaces   85

Chapter 11: Opportunities for New Forms of Living   91

Chapter 12: Child-Friendly Districts   101

Chapter 13: Air and Noise Pollution   107

Part III: Climate Adaptation and Nature — 119

Chapter 14: Green Space — 121

Chapter 15: Sponge Cities and Water Loops — 127

Chapter 16: Active Resilience with Passive House — 133

Chapter 17: The Heat Is Already Here — 143

Part IV: Building Decarbonization — 157

Chapter 18: Circular Mass Timber Districts — 159

Chapter 19: Decarbonized Buildings — 167

Chapter 20: Futureproofing with Open Building — 173

Epilogue: Unleashing Brilliant Futures — 177
Notes — 183
About the Author — 197

Foreword

Urbanism in the Planetary Crisis

By Alex Steffen

Our cities are not ready for the planetary crisis now unfolding around us.

Mike Eliason wants to help you change that.

The fundamental reality of urbanism in the twenty-first century is that the systems and places we've made are no longer suited to the chaotic planet on which we now live. In the next decades, every city on Earth will have to contend with extremes of heat, drought, rainfall, and wind those cities have never before experienced. At the same time, they'll be forced to plan their paths forward through economic and social upheavals, from loss of insurability to resource constraints to mass displacement. Conventional North American assumptions about urban governance and planning have not prepared any of us for this task. We are caught in the midst of a discontinuity. Past education, expertise, and experience are no longer useful guides to future decisions.

Cities that want to thrive amid this chaos must do three things: grow faster, work better, and ruggedize themselves. Ecodistricts, Eliason shows us, offer high-leverage tools for doing all three.

Grow Faster

Many North American cities already suffer serious housing shortages. This is merely prelude to the challenges to come. The harsh truth of our moment is that millions of people will soon find themselves on the move as the places they live suffer worsening climate and ecological damages, experience prolonged economic downturns, and offer dwindling prospects to the people who live there. We are unprepared for the magnitude of future housing demand in cities whose relatively safe climates and comparative wealth position them to more easily weather the worsening storms of the twenty-first century.

We can't suppress housing demand. It doesn't work, short of violence. We've seen again and again that cities refusing to build sufficient housing despite

Alex Steffen is an award-winning writer and one of the world's leading practitioners of climate foresight. His newsletter and podcast can be found at thesnapforward.com.

rising demand may force some people to leave the area, but mostly they simply push residents into marginal conditions: People are forced into hyper-commutes from distant suburbs, crowded into expensive rentals (and cut off from the financial stability that comes from homeownership), or simply driven into homelessness.

The solution to inadequate supply, both empirical research and common sense suggest, is to build more housing. Yet there are limits to the number of homes that can be built using incremental infill strategies and costs to confining our dense housing to polluted arterial corridors. The answer to these problems is to build at district scales.

District developments allow us to amass a lot of new housing and workplaces in smart ways, folding in sustainability solutions from the start. Combined with architectural and planning practices that are already working elsewhere, such as green infrastructure, point access blocks, pedestrianized streetscapes, collective building, Passive House designs, net zero energy systems, mass timber, and other new materials, districts enable new projects that actively improve their neighborhoods.

By the middle of the century, successful cities will almost certainly be the ones that build enough housing to manage the influx of climate migrants and refugees and the ongoing demands of current residents and their children and grandchildren. That means districts and lots of them.

Work Better

Beset as we are with personal worries and moral concerns about our worsening ecological future, we tend not to understand that this crisis is not an issue, like other issues, that we can work together to "solve." It is, instead, a new era. It is the context in which all material decisions are now being made. Therefore, many of its greatest near-term effects will be disruptive economically rather than apocalyptic ecologically. We're in a time of convulsive changes in the global economy.

Building the cities we need—in effective ways, on equitable terms, and at the necessary pace—will be neither easy nor cheap. That build demands nothing short of a reboot of our regional and local economies to meet new global realities. It demands policies and plans and investments to spur the new industries and jobs needed in our new chaotic circumstances.

Production, Eliason reminds us, is at the core of urban purpose. Cities that invent the things we need to live well with new realities—that design them, make them (or grow them), and sell them—have futures.

On the most basic level, this involves cities where citizens turn their businesses and industries to catch the rising wind of decarbonization and sustainable prosperity. However, the future economy is evolving fast and will go on transforming for decades. Cities must grow adept not just at providing the new but at continuing to find the next new. This will require not just research hubs or professional communities but also productive districts and adaptable land uses where complex networks of people working in different disciplines and industries can fuel each other's acceleration. It takes making spaces for the new to reveal itself. Districts, Eliason shows, can be built as platforms for making that happen.

Ruggedize

We underestimate how much hardship is in store even in places that are relatively safe, as long as they fail to prepare for climate and ecological upheavals. Cities will need to pursue ruggedization—the proactive and generative avoidance of collapse—if they hope to thrive.

Climate adaptation measures are a key component of these ruggedization efforts. Sometimes this means megaprojects, such as putting in new water supply infrastructure or building large wetlands to protect shorelines from storms and tidal surges. But much of the work will (of necessity) be done at more local and granular scales. That's where, as Eliason shows, districts again can shine.

Districts provide the opportunity to deploy adaptation solutions across large areas, such as using green spaces as "sponges" to control flooding or planting street trees to lessen the local impacts of heatwaves. But better-designed buildings, compact development, and innovative infrastructure can also make districts better able to resist interruptions, by, for instance, ensuring the capacities of residents to maintain healthy and comfortable conditions even during power outages or in the wake of disasters. Adaptation is good, but passive durability is better.

Neither is the real payoff for district-scale innovations, though. Much of our thinking about preparing our communities for climate chaos has centered on the idea of making costly investments to preserve a continuity of functions, a loss we suffer to reduce future losses. However, districts can turn the need for preparation into a vehicle for increased prosperity and growing capacities.

They can save residents money, sure, and help maintain the insurability and credit-worthiness of their surrounding communities. But they can also attract new businesses and talent and local investment—and provide the workers, ideas, and resources their cities need to reinvent, restructure, and retrofit themselves. By concentrating housing, opportunities, and more durable livable systems, districts can do far more than change the land on which they sit. They can help cities reweave the broader urban fabric, even when the city as a whole is stuck changing more slowly than it ought to.

Finally, there's quality of life. One of the most hopeful realities of sustainable urbanism is that the solutions cities use to grow faster, work better, and ruggedize themselves for the future all reinforce each other. Done right, these interwoven solutions contribute to a higher quality of life. Reducing the centrality of cars in our neighborhoods, for example, lets us shrink the proportion of roads and parking to parks and homes, lessening flood risk, cooling communities, and reducing emissions. It also can mean places that welcome children, that offer clean air, quiet, and shade.

The evidence suggests that a huge number of Americans and Canadians want to live affordable, productive lives in rugged and sustainable communities. That we are not building such communities does not reflect popular demand but rather (as Eliason shows) reveals a whole series of planning policy and code failures. We've broken the systems that build our cities, and we're going to need to find a way back. In coming years, nearly everyone involved with city-making is going to be looking for new approaches to tackle interwoven urban problems, under climate pressures, and on an uncomfortably rapid timeline.

This book offers an invitation to imagining the powerful possibilities to be found between the denial and inertia of contemporary planning and the dreary insubstantiality of utopian urban dreams. Districts are very likely to be where the future gets built.

Preface

From 2003 to 2004, I had the privilege of living and working in the German city of Freiburg, a medium-sized university town nestled at the edge of the Black Forest, in the southwest corner where Germany borders Switzerland and France. The firm, Pfeifer Roser Kuhn Architekten, was doing incredibly innovative and forward-thinking work with mass timber and low-energy buildings, at a very formative time in my career.

In many ways, it wasn't *working* in Freiburg that transformed my life but rather *living* in this awe-inducing city. Freiburg's historic core is a massive car-free pedestrian zone where trams, pedestrians, and cyclists have priority instead of being inundated with cars, as in most North American cities. Freiburg bills itself as "a city of short distances" and is well connected by tram and bus lines, with a safe and solid bicycle network. The ease of mobility, of living without a car, after spending most of the preceding years in auto-centric towns and cities, was unheard of. I ended up living in a small attic apartment in the pedestrian zone. To this day, the middle of the bustling Altstadt (old city) is the quietest and most fascinating place I have ever lived.

Freiburg's periphery includes a number of well-planned, moderately dense districts that were completely foreign to anything covered in my professional education stateside. These include the districts of Vauban and Rieselfeld, which are well known in planning circles today but were nearly unheard of twenty years ago. Vauban, a wonderfully quiet, family-friendly, lush, and car-light ecodistrict features numerous Baugruppen and other innovative forms of collective housing. Rieselfeld, planned almost concurrently with Vauban, is much more diverse and urban—and fascinating in its own right. These two districts were both finishing construction at the time and contained a number of planning principles that have since become distilled in my own thinking about cities, nature, housing, livability, quality of life, and climate adaptation.

In a small café on an early afternoon in fall of 2003, I ended up meeting an incredible, intelligent woman whom I would eventually marry. We now have two kids, no car, several bikes and cargo bikes—and have spent much of the last twenty years trying to graft aspects and values that we picked up from our time in Freiburg into our daily lives in Seattle. This has included trying to build our own mass timber and Passive House Baugruppe, something that has been quite challenging due to high costs and low-quality construction.

In 2019, I founded Larch Lab because I wanted to focus more on research, policy, and advocacy for climate adaptive development and to push housing in the United States to be more in line with what is built in other countries, such as Japan, Mexico, and (naturally) Germany. The way we build and plan development in the United States is very different from these places. Multi-family housing in the United States is far inferior to single-family housing, but this isn't the case in other places. The way we build has incredibly negative effects related to climate adaptation, public health, and community. This book aims to bring to the forefront how we can develop livable, low-carbon places by looking at models and projects outside our own country.

Acknowledgments

I would like to thank the numerous people who supported and mentored me through this process. Without you this book would not exist.

To my editor at Island Press, Heather Boyer, for quickly grasping the vision and helping me see this to fruition. To Derek Sagehorn, for prodding me to write this book and help change the discussion around development and housing in the United States. I would also like to thank the architects, planners, and photographers who allowed their art to be incorporated in this book; it is so much better because of you. To Alex Steffen, for encouraging me to think about how climate change will affect people, buildings, and cities in the future.

To the entire Passive House community, who on a daily basis obsessively think about buildings, climate, and energy more than anyone else on Earth, including Dr. Wolfgang Feist, Bronwyn Barry, Monte Paulsen, Ken Levenson, and Shaun St-Amour.

To Matthew Grocoff at THRIVE Collaborative, for quickly grasping my "housing theory of everything" and helping to spread the ideas that turned into this book. To Markus Neuber at ALN, for showing me that architecture should be fun, being an incredible boss and colleague, and giving my family the opportunity to raise our kids in Germany.

I would also like to thank Lloyd Alter, for constantly pushing me to write and offering opportunities to spread my ideas. To Jay Stoeckel, whose memory looms large, and who taught me to keep looking. To Hunter Pittman and Steven Thompson, who actually convinced a farmer to let students design and build his rammed earth house and pushed us to think outside the box.

To my friends—Aaron, Gene, Nick, Greg, Pete, and the rest of the dadball crew—not only are you always quick with a joke, but I would not have made it through the pandemic without you. Please note that I ignored all of your book title suggestions.

To my parents, Bill and Debbie, for raising us in places where we were constantly challenged, never letting me stop asking why, and fostering a lifelong pursuit of intellect and curiosity. To Leslie Eliason, whose interests and life in Seattle influenced mine, and whom I wish I could have known as an adult.

Lastly, none of this would have been possible without my incredible wife, Heather Eliason, along with Clementine and Sebastian, who always provide wonderful insights and humor. Thank you for making the space to take on this project (and countless others), for our bicycle and travel adventures, for always pushing us to live our values and leave this world a better place, and for making a life with me.

Introduction

"Moreover, modern housing provides certain minimum amenities for every dwelling: cross-ventilation, for one thing; sunlight, quiet, and a pleasant outlook from every window."

—Catherine Bauer, *Modern Housing*

Nearly ninety years after housing advocate Catherine Bauer penned that line in *Modern Housing*, I have begun to think it may have been one of the most prescient in her book. The way housing and neighborhoods are built in the United States today is a radical departure, one where dwellings often do not have sunlight, are not quiet, do not have pleasant outlooks, and do not have the ability to cross-ventilate. This departure begins with something as simple and mundane as requirements for multiple stairs and a corridor connecting them, a requirement rarely found for most urban housing the world over. It ends with new districts oriented around transit with little affordable housing, poorly planned urban realms that are incredibly autocentric in the very types of places they shouldn't be. The disparity in resulting outcomes could not be more significant. Our regulations result in housing that is less livable, less climate adaptive, and less family-friendly, and with a much lower quality of life.

As a practicing architect, I never considered that our building and planning codes could be detrimental to addressing the very things I have been focused on from a personal and professional standpoint: livable cities, building decarbonization, and climate adaptation. After numerous years researching building codes and their effects on buildings, and spending a few years working in Germany, I believe that we could vastly improve the way buildings and neighborhoods are planned in the United States and Canada to be more livable and adaptive to a changing climate by rethinking how we plan and regulate our buildings to be thinner and more family friendly. I believe that our own processes and approaches leave little opportunity to achieve the types of neighborhoods that planners, politicians, and architects flock to when abroad. But I am hopeful this book can provide an insight into the potential that development approaches and models found outside the United States, such as ecodistricts, can offer.

The United Nations predicts that nearly 70 percent of the global population will live in cities and urbanized areas in 2050. In my own city, Seattle, a recent Microsoft report stated we had a housing deficit of 194,000 homes. Recent estimates from Freddie Mac showed a national housing shortage of 3.8 million homes. We have growing housing affordability crises across nearly all economic spectra. In 2023, Canada had its first year with a population increase exceeding one million residents, and its population is expected to double in less than twenty-five years. That is an incredible amount of housing that needs to be built. How and where it will be built will have a sizable effect on carbon emissions. Will we choose to build dense, livable, low-carbon ecodistricts? Or will we see massive amounts of carbon lock-in with continued patterns of unsustainable sprawl?

Many of the topics in recent housing discourse—office-to-residential conversions, micro units, windowless bedrooms, missing middle housing—are largely a reaction to a century of incredibly poor building and land use regulation, including exclusionary zoning that banned all forms of collective housing. With the rise in postpandemic work from home, office-to-residential conversions are being explored as a way to correct decades of a poor mix of uses in downtown cores. However, because of cheap energy and a lack of daylighting requirements, modern office buildings have incredibly deep floor plates, making it difficult to get functional apartments and incredibly expensive to rehabilitate them. Windowless bedrooms are a function of a building code in much of the United States that allows them (although many countries, and cities such as New York and San Francisco do not), yielding deep, bowling-lane-shaped single-aspect dwellings that have windows on only one side. Micro units are a means of getting more dwellings that are slightly less expensive to rent in buildings that are significantly larger in virtually any metric (e.g., floor area, density, volume) than in peer countries. Much of the land area of US cities is filled with detached houses, a function of a century of exclusionary zoning.

That lack of flexibility, of poor foresight, can be found in numerous aspects of US and Canadian cities. In sprawling suburbs where development patterns and street layouts severely constrain walkability or mobility. In poorly zoned neighborhoods that do not have much, if any, economic and social mix of residents. In transit-oriented density (TOD) that is incredibly autocentric, loud, and offering a poorer quality of life than it should.

Aerial photo of Sonnwendviertel in Vienna, a 77-acre car-light ecodistrict planned for 13,000 residents and 20,000 jobs. (Credit: Christian Fürthner)

Over the last decade, I have been grappling with a number of questions about how urban environments can be transformed to be more inclusive and affordable and to do so in a way that offers a high quality of life while being adaptive to a changing climate. In this search, I have come to realize that there are underlying aspects to *how* we plan, dictated by codes and standards and affecting myriad issues in unseen ways. Part of my work at Larch Lab has been to highlight what these differences are, working with legislators, housing advocates, architects, and planners to advocate for changes to allow for better buildings. Our current paradigm not only affects the *types* of housing we can build but the *quality* of that housing. During a presentation in New Zealand, a colleague commented that even if one were to visit new urban districts in other countries, such as Vauban or Vienna's Sonnwendviertel, it would be really difficult to get a sense of how interconnected things are because the underlying codes are not readily grasped. They compared this with visiting Ghent, Belgium, which has seen a dramatic mobility transition, and seeing or understanding the dimensions and configurations of transformed streets or bicycle lanes. It is virtually impossible to experience

Introduction xix

the Circulation Plan that redirects traffic around the city center and induces the use of more sustainable modes of transportation.

In a sense, this book is intended as a way of seeing how these things are all connected: climate adaptation, buildings, livable neighborhoods, decarbonization, sustainable mobility, public health, and quality of life. Of understanding and overcoming how our own regulations and processes can prevent and stifle the very places the planning profession, developers, and politicians claim they want to create. It captures the answers to many of the fundamental questions that I have asked over the many years of working on creating more livable, affordable, low-carbon cities.

What would it be like to live in a car-light or car-free neighborhood? Why does American TOD look nothing like European TOD? What could climate adaptive neighborhoods look like? What if we had more options for housing beyond the binary of rented apartments and owned houses and townhomes? Can neighborhoods become carbon sinks?

This book will help clarify how the processes, regulations, and prioritization of public health and quality of life work together to create livable, low-carbon communities. It is divided into four sections: planning the ecodistrict, quality of life and public health, climate adaptation and nature, and building decarbonization. This manual is intended for both new and existing neighborhood retrofits and building-level construction. I bring together a number of topics to show that not only is it possible to build better housing and neighborhoods, but it is imperative. We can build better housing. We can build up community. We can build places able to withstand the worsening effects of climate change. We can provide affordable housing in urban areas for families and workers. We can make space for jobs. As cities pivot postpandemic to address both systemic housing shortages and a worsening climate crisis, scale and flexibility will become paramount to addressing both of these issues simultaneously. But we cannot wait; it is time to deliver.

CHAPTER 1

The Compact, Climate Adaptive Ecodistrict

"We must shift our thinking away from short-term gain toward long-term investment and sustainability, and always have the next generations in mind with every decision we make."

—Deb Haaland, Secretary, US Department of Interior

We, as a species, have to learn to think differently.

The ongoing and devastating events of the polycrisis[1] are interwoven and interconnected in frightening ways: the lingering effects of COVID, a worsening affordable housing shortage, a social isolation and loneliness crisis,[2] climate change, and more. The postwar patterns of development in the United States, with sprawl being omnipresent among them, have in many ways exacerbated these crises.

What if cities prioritized climate adaptive neighborhoods with abundant affordable housing, open space, and people-centered places, offering a high quality of life, with good jobs and the ability to adapt to a changing climate? Neighborhoods focused on high-quality living, with the daily amenities that can be accessed without cars? Places that are lush with gardens, courtyards, playgrounds? Districts that are multigenerational, child friendly, and even quiet? In many European and Asian cities these are exactly the types of places being developed. Cervero and Sullivan call this green transit-oriented development (TOD),[3] but I prefer the term *ecodistricts*, short for *ecologically oriented districts*. Ecodistricts offer the possibility of broadly addressing the polycrisis: neighborhoods of respite and adaptation to a changing climate. Places that are community oriented and social, to blunt the effects of the social isolation crisis. Places where a broad mix of housing types and tenures allows for a broad mix of residents, addressing the growing housing crises affecting our cities. The Organisation for Economic Co-operation and Development defines the eco-neighbourhood as "an urban neighbourhood designed to have minimal environmental impact by achieving sustainable resource management of energy, water and waste; dense and mixed-use development; and less automobile dependency supported by public transport systems, walking and biking."[4]

The eco-city and eco-neighborhood concepts have been a growing global phenomenon, with several realized and planned projects since the 2000s.[5] There is abundant potential for these types of places to be built and retrofitted in US and Canadian cities and suburbs, learning from the exemplary districts happening around the world.

Freiburg's Vauban and Malmö's Bo01 are oft-cited examples. In Freiburg, I saw what is possible in redeveloping brownfields into socially mixed, ecologically focused urban districts. Brownfield development is critical, because cities already have ample room to develop, repair, and reconnect without building new cities in greenfields disconnected from existing infrastructure. Hamburg might have the best motto to highlight this approach: "Mehr Stadt in der Stadt" ("More city within the city"). They have designated 80 percent of new development to be located in the city, rather than in greenfields outside the existing built-up area.[6]

France requires ecological urban development primarily on brownfields with its ÉcoQuartier (Écologique, "ecological," and *Quartier*, "district") label, which passed into law in 2012. The French Ministry of Ecological Transition defines an ÉcoQuartier as "a development project that integrates the issues and principles of the city and sustainable territories."[7] The ÉcoQuartier label is used in numerous cities and villages across France, across a variety of scales, from a hundred homes all the way up to several thousand. Proximity and diversity of functions, participatory planning, and social inclusion are all central to the label's scoring.

There has been a push for ecodistricts in the United States, with the Portland-based nonprofit EcoDistricts that developed the Protocols, a program designed for "a new model of urban regeneration to empower just, resilient, sustainable neighborhoods for all."[8] The organization was founded to bring best practices to the neighborhood and district scales with a focus on equity, resilience, and climate protection. It has focused largely on the incremental regeneration of existing urban neighborhoods, in contrast to Europe, which tends to focus on new or redeveloped neighborhoods. Rehabilitating existing neighborhoods to be more climate adaptive and equitable is significantly more difficult, and although it is not the focus of this book, it is incredibly important. Seattle's Capitol Hill Ecodistrict was the first certified ecodistrict in that Pacific Northwest,[9] which had largely been achieved in an existing dense, vibrant neighborhood. In 2021, EcoDistricts was incorporated into the Partnership for Southern Equity, with the program renamed Just Communities.[10]

Small-Scale Urban Development

There is a lack of granularity in US development today that is found in the historical patterns of development. Blocks in historic neighborhoods contain multiple different parcels, often with different owners. As those blocks are redeveloped and reintensified, small-scale projects are no longer possible, and parcel assemblage is required. Small-scale urban development in

Aurora Avenue, a state highway bisecting Seattle, with development capacity for nearly 100,000 homes. (Credit: Michael Eliason)

4 Building for People

the United States is really limited to buildings of three stories or less. As described in Chapter 6, this is primarily due to building codes, planning codes, and finance regimes that in effect require significantly larger and deeper buildings. However, this is not the case for new development in many other countries, as their planning allows for small, fine-grained development that can be used in both new and historic neighborhoods. One city that does this really well is Freiburg.

Although this book focuses on larger developments, these concepts and strategies can be used in smaller ones as well.

Currently, Freiburg is planning a new ecodistrict on the periphery of the city, called Dietenbach. Dietenbach is split into separate quarters, each containing several semipermeable perimeter blocks. The city is specifically aiming for *staedtebaulichen Kleinteiligkeit*, or small-scale urban development at the block level. The city is doing this for a number of reasons but primarily "in order to generate varied and lively building structures, which also enable mixture of different uses & have a high degree of adaptability to future structural changes." They are specifically aiming to avoid the banality of large postwar estates or contemporary development, in order to allow a more mixed, vibrant, and varied streetscape.[11]

Top left: Courtyard path through a semi-permeable perimeter block in Freiburg's Rieselfeld district. (Credit: Payton Chung)

Left: Aerial photo of Freiburg's Rieselfeld district, showing how thin buildings allow for massive private and semi-public courtyards. (Credit: Volker Jung)

Right: Historic pattern of development in Landshut, Germany, reflecting small scale walkable urbanism (Credit: Michael Eliason)

The Compact, Climate Adaptive Ecodistrict 5

Building on the experience of previous neighborhoods, proposed regulations in Dietenbach would induce a diverse and mixed district, even at the block level. Blocks would be composed of different-sized parcels, generally a minimum of eight, although several would have more. In order to ensure a broad variety of housing types and tenures, each block would contain four of six different housing types on the Development Framework Plan. These housing types are attached small-plexes, four-plexes with stacked flats, small apartment buildings of five to eight dwellings, medium apartment buildings

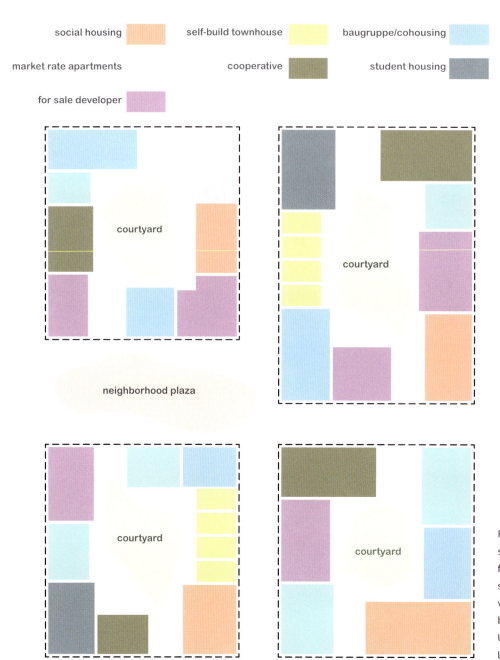

Regulations that allow small scale urban development allow for a greater economic and social mix at the block level, versus one or two massive buildings as is typical in the US. (Credit: Michael Eliason/ Larch Lab)

6 Building for People

with ten to twenty dwellings, and large apartments of more than thirty dwellings. This typological and ownership mix would ensure a broad economic and social mix of residents, rare in US development. Developers would also be limited to a maximum of forty dwellings per block, on at most two parcels per block.[12] This would enable a broad diversity of tenure at the block level, as well as housing including apartments, condos, social housing, cooperatives, and Baugruppen (German for "building group," self-developed urban housing similar to cohousing). Instead of a development trying to look like several smaller ones through modulation or a messy material mix, the development would be separate buildings. This is exactly as we used to build in US cities but forgot along the way.

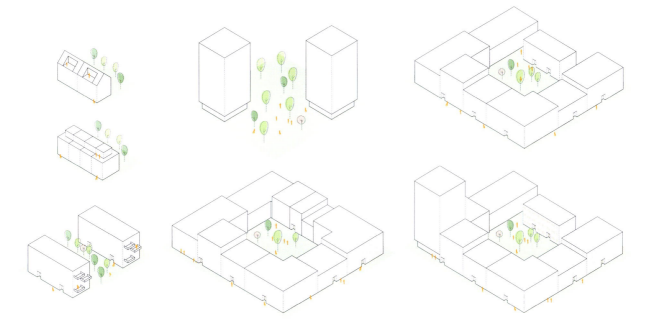

Building regulations play a strong role in the production and variety of building forms including semi-detached houses, rowhouses, slab buildings (zeilenbauten), perimeter blocks, point towers (punkthaeuser), or hybrids of these. (Credit: Michael Eliason/Larch Lab)

On Form

Ecodistricts come in a variety of scales, from small settlements of a few acres with a hundred homes to massive projects such as Dietenbach or Hamburg's Oberbillwerder, planning for 7,000 homes on 292 acres. The urban form can range from almost pastoral to incredibly dense, with towers and midrise buildings spanning for blocks, up to a half mile from a transit station.

Pound for pound, the midrise building of four to eight stories is one of the most effective and appropriate for compact, walkable development. An analysis by the City of Berlin found that buildings containing five stories, including an inhabited attic, had virtually the same residential density as buildings greater than ten stories.

The Compact, Climate Adaptive Ecodistrict 7

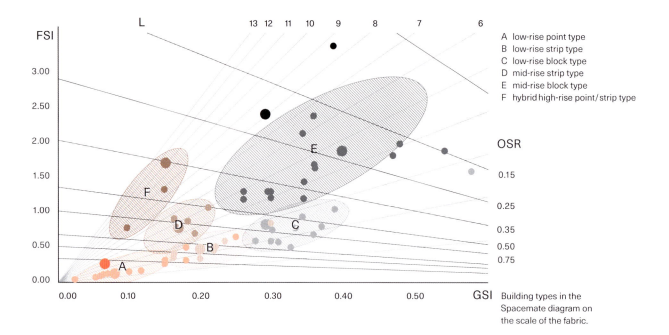

Building types in the Spacemate diagram on the scale of the fabric.

The form of development at the block level also plays a role in urban character, density, and climate adaptability. The dense urban perimeter blocks found in the historic cores of cities such as Paris, Vienna, and Amsterdam allow for an incredible amount of density without much height. Alternatively, the urban form of Hong Kong or Singapore's towers allows for a significant amount of density over very little land but may not be the most resilient, as climate-change-induced events such as wildfires or heat events result in power outages that prevent elevator usage. US land use codes generally only look at floor area ratio (FAR), the ratio of the allowed building area on a given site divided by the site area. There are numerous other issues that can be considered, such as lot coverage (the percentage of lot occupied by building).

When it comes to urban form, there are several options, although in the United States they tend to not play a role in urban planning. These are detached buildings, rowhouses, slab buildings, perimeter blocks, and towers in the park—and then there are hybrids combining aspects of these. The urban housing types all have a different character to them, but the perimeter block is one with the most character. It also provides for much more open space, density, and interesting opportunities for mixed-use urbanity.

Spacemate is a visualization tool for understanding the relationships between density, open space, and urban form developed by Meta Berghauser Pont and Per Haupt that looks at FAR, lot coverage, the number of floors, the

The Spacemate is a matrix designed to help visualize the connections between open space, Floor Area Ratio (FSI), and building height (L) at the block level. Midrise blocks stand out as the superfruit of walkable urbanism, allowing for optimal levels of proximity, open space, and density. (Credit: Meta Burghauser Pont)

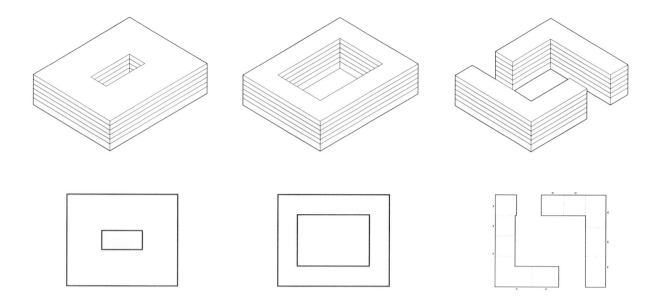

Diagram comparing amount of open or green space the typical US perimeter block with an 80-foot-deep double loaded corridor (left), a closed European style perimeter block with a 45-foot-deep floor plate (middle), and a semi-permeable perimeter block with varied building depths up to 45 feet (right). (Credit: Michael Eliason/Larch Lab)

amount of open space at ground level, and network effects.[13] When I first saw this diagram in 2009, I could not get my head around why perimeter blocks and super blocks scored so much better than high rises, and then it hit me: It was the compactness *paired* with open space. It took me a few more years to realize that the increase in open space was directly related to thinner buildings, with more stories than typical in the United States, but this was just part of the picture. The key was figuring out what enabled the buildings to be thinner in the first place; as described in Chapter 5, this key is point access blocks.

The perimeter block composed of thin and tall buildings is ideally situated for compact urban development. It allows for a high degree of livability, dwellings with views and daylight on multiple sides, family-sized homes, and larger courtyards to congregate in and mitigate urban heat islands and stormwater. The perimeter block allows more dwellings to have good solar access while allowing for moderate levels of privacy. It orients buildings to the street and quieter courtyard, as opposed to neighbors a few feet away. It has better daylight exposure than most other urban types as well.[14] Because of its compact nature, it also tends to have a lower heating demand than other building forms, which tends to decrease with building height.[15]

More restricted airflow is a noted negative effect, but a solution to this that I rather like is the semipermeable perimeter block. A semipermeable perimeter block includes gaps that increase daylight, airflow, and views. Airflow is going to become a larger issue in dealing with overheating from climate change, so allowing for some level of permeability will be increasingly important.

The Compact, Climate Adaptive Ecodistrict   9

Height is often a point of contention in development in US cities. The four- to eight-story block structure allows for a wide variety of housing and tenure types and an optimal level of density for walkability. However, mixing in the occasional taller building or tower can help balance out more density and provide accent points within the district. Variability in height not only is visually interesting but allows for increased views and daylight over conventional perimeter blocks.[16] It is also something better achieved with small-scale urban development, as opposed to massive block-sized projects. Skyscrapers in the mix can also work, but when it comes to climate adaptability and resilience and issues of embodied carbon, they score low on these metrics.

Toward Compact, Integrated Ecodistricts

The integrally planned ecodistrict will have an abundance of open and green space, future-oriented mobility, and climate adaptation measures to allow a good life in economically and socially mixed neighborhoods. In aiming for livable, low-carbon districts, it is imperative that the whole is greater than the sum of its parts, and the parts are arranged through a climate lens. Livability is related not only to climate adaptation but to public health and quality of life. The ecodistrict should offer a quality of life as high as, if not higher than, that found in detached houses. Canadian urban planner Brent Toderian notes that cities should "be unashamed to have a consistently high urban design standard."[17] These are fundamentally human-scaled places, with a good mix of uses and necessities of life within reach. Cities that adopt these measures will set an example that urban expansion and contraction can be livable, sustainable, and more affordable than today's inequitable status quo. The opportunities in the compact, climate adaptive ecodistrict are numerous and include the following:

- a functional mix of uses, community spaces, schools, shops, grocery stores, cafes, restaurants, and other amenities needed for daily life (Chapters 6, 9, and 10);
- the productive city, including space for work such as office spaces, workshops, co-working spaces, and even space for industry (Chapter 3);
- energy efficiency, carbon emission accounting, energy flows, and water flows to enable efficient, low-carbon living (Chapters 4, 15, 16, and 18);
- space for living and working in places that are more adaptable to the extreme and unpredictable weather events associated with climate change (Chapters 5, 15 and 17);
- more future-proof and flexible ways of building, with new low-carbon

technologies that result in better, more durable, and more livable homes (Chapters 18, 19, and 20);

- a broad array of housing, for more inclusivity and affordability, with new forms of living (Chapters 9, 11 and 12);

- car-light living encouraged by the prioritization of sustainable mobility and a high-quality public realm (Chapters 8 and 10);

- better public health outcomes, due to reductions in air and noise pollution (Chapter 13);

- innovative, inclusive, and future-oriented forms of co-participation and planning procedures (Chapters 6 and 7).

Pivoting toward the future of sustainable urban development, cities need to prioritize livable, climate adaptive places offering car-light and car-free living, affordable housing, and much more access to green and open space. The chapters in this book highlight several themes that must be prioritized to make these places a reality. Although this book is intended for compact urban development, the concepts and ideas found within are just as applicable to suburban districts, as well as individual buildings, both new and adapted. Architects, planners, developers, owners, institutions, insurers, and politicians must start thinking about how climate in the future will affect their buildings and how their portfolios can be rapidly adapted to these drastic changes. Our buildings were designed for a climate that no longer exists; the impacts will range from incredibly uncomfortable to increasingly deadly. The sooner we come to terms with this, the sooner we might begin to pivot toward a better and more sustainable future.

CHAPTER 2

Rethinking Urban Development in the United States

There are effectively two patterns of dense urban development in North American cities, and although both may slightly reduce carbon emissions, neither offers livable, green places. The first is reintensification of areas already zoned for commerce and multifamily housing. Often, this entails upzoning, or increasing the allowed intensity of development, on sites that largely already have existing housing or businesses. These repeated cycles of upzoning induce a sort of urban cannibalism, destroying the very places that give a neighborhood a soul, identity, and character. Because of modern building and planning regulations, those existing buildings are replaced with significantly larger ones that often take up much or all of a block. These rezoned areas typically are found along major arterials and highways, which are also some of the most toxic places found in cities.[1]

The detrimental effects of this type of development could be lessened if planners and politicians would allow moderate levels of density far off the arterials. Although there is significant demand for walkable neighborhoods like those found in historic US neighborhoods or places such as Mexico City, Tokyo, or Berlin, limiting walkable density to narrow swaths of the city rather than broad areas curtails the character found in those types of neighborhoods. It also ensures that the amenities associated with walkable neighborhoods are largely accessible only to those who can afford to live in or near them. The challenge is that this unhealthy pattern of reintensification on arterials occurs because cities restrict new multifamily housing and urban development in most urban areas. The land area of nearly every US city is overwhelmingly zoned for detached houses.[2] This is slowly changing, as cities and states have realized the existing paradigm is no longer tenable and work to preempt their decades-old codes and processes. The entire west coast has effectively eliminated exclusionary zoning, at least in name, and is slowly adding new forms of housing including missing middle housing. As defined by Opticos Design's Daniel Parolek, missing middle housing is small-scale housing types, from one to three stories, that are compatible with detached single-family homes, such as duplexes, triplexes, rowhouses,

In Seattle, as in most of the United States, dense multifamily development including transit-oriented development (TOD) is largely relegated along noisy and polluted arterials and highways, resulting in low levels of walkability in poor-quality places. (Credit: Luke Gardner)

garden court apartments, and live–work buildings.[3] These forms of housing are missing, as they were zoned out of existence for most residentially zoned urban land starting in the 1920s and 1930s.

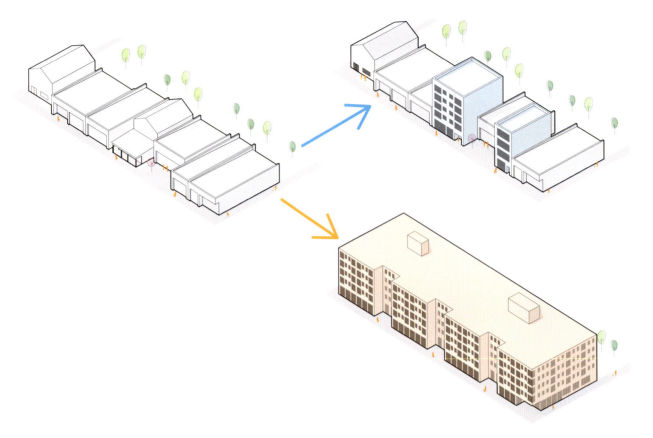

The second development pattern, which has seen an increase in numerous US and Canadian cities, is transit-oriented development (TOD). In 1993, planner Peter Calthorpe coined the term, writing, "The TOD concept is simple: moderate and high-density housing, along with complementary public uses, jobs, retail and services, are concentrated in mixed-use developments at strategic points along the regional transit system."[4] TOD has become a common planning approach in the United States, with the Center for Neighborhood Technology noting there are currently over 6,000 TOD locations built or in planning.[5]

Although TOD in the United States is usually adjacent to transit and may even be walkable, it generally has not prioritized climate adaptive communities to the degree needed. However, this is starting to change, as cities realize that there is demand for places that offer a high quality of life and push the boundaries beyond today's unsustainable status quo. Park space is surprisingly limited in TOD. Most TOD does not have a high level of affordable housing and therefore lacks a broad social and economic mix of residents.

Building regulations affect development or redevelopment patterns. The US requirement for two or more stairs leads to significantly larger buildings (orange) than in places where point access blocks (blue) and small-scale urban development are allowed. (Credit: Michael Eliason/Larch Lab)

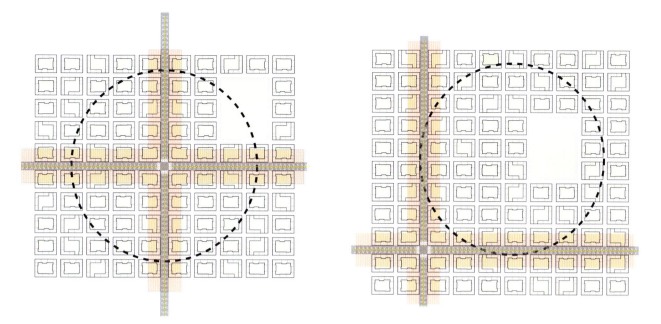

Locating ecodistricts or TOD adjacent to or off arterials, instead of centering on them, allows for higher-quality neighborhoods where fewer residents or businesses are exposed to high levels of air and noise pollution. (Credit: Michael Eliason/Larch Lab)

High-quality public spaces are rare, generally limited to retail-oriented places. There is an opportunity to rethink how existing urban brownfields can be redeveloped to be climate adaptive, affordable ecodistricts with a mix of uses and housing types.

Reassessing Automobility

The goal of TOD should be to facilitate day-to-day living without the need for cars, to allow for high-quality low-carbon living with radical reductions in car usage and associated public health issues. Unfortunately, TOD is still incredibly autocentric, with abundant on- and off-street parking, wide streets, and massive buildings. Research has shown that although TOD reduces vehicle usage rates by as much as 35 percent,[6] it still tends to be overparked, with a 2020 Stark-Portage Area Computer Consortium report noting, "The 'over-parking' of projects near transit probably plays a large part in explaining why some TODs in the U.S. have failed to meet expectations for transit ridership gains and congestion reductions."[7] A recently announced mixed-use TOD project in the suburbs of Salt Lake City, Utah, with a projected 7,400 homes and space for 30,000 jobs, claimed it was aiming for a "15 Minute City." This same district will have space for an eye-popping 40,800 parking spaces.[8] In addition, TOD that is not as walkable and pedestrian oriented as it could be is noted for a decrease in car ownership but an *increase* in ride-hailing,[9] potentially negating the effects of reduced ownership.

Cities sometimes limit TOD to as little as one block off loud, dangerous arterials, which isn't conducive to walkable, livable environments. Open space often feels like an afterthought. "Complete Streets," where road space is given for all modes while prioritizing none, instead of prioritizing sustainable mobility, are quite frequently implemented.

TOD is not normally designed for families, and even schools may not be walkable from or within a station area. Even if the district is designed for them, children can find it difficult to access parks or playgrounds without having to cross one or more streets. Building codes and development financing result in few family-sized homes. Affordable housing is often relegated to a handful of token projects and rarely to the percentage found near transit in other countries.

Quality of Life

The United Nations Weight of Cities report recommends cities to "develop appealing mixed-use and socially mixed inner-city neighbourhoods: These should be attractive and therefore remove the incentive to invest in the urbanization of the suburbs, focusing development instead around high-access 'nodes' of the transport network."[10] In the years that I have been researching ecodistricts and TOD, discussions oriented around the social mix, appealing

Freiburg's Rieselfeld is centered on a tram line with adequate bike connections and traffic-calmed streets, allowing for a much quieter district than TOD focused on arterials. (Credit: Payton Chung)

16 Building for People

Courtyards that offer space for living, as in Stockholm's Hammarby Sjöstad, seem a much better option than parking. (Credit: Alex Linthicum)

places, and a high quality of life are far more prevalent in Europe. The outcomes tend to reflect that focus as well. Part of this difference is related to US building and planning codes that result in less livable buildings. These codes, paired with our construction practices, result in multifamily housing that offers a significantly worse quality of life than single-family houses, whereas this is not necessarily the case in other countries.

In Germany, "Wie wollen wir im Morgen leben?" ("How do we want to live together tomorrow?") is a constant refrain heard around neighborhood development. Co-creation was rooted in the ecodistrict of Vauban's planning and realization. Districts are planned to shield traffic noise, as opposed to being centered on highways or arterials. There is a much broader diversity in housing tenure and type, allowing for a much better economic and social mix of residents. European districts tend to be laden with space for community, nature, and culture. High-quality urban planning is almost always a central focus, and there is significant demand and potential for these same kinds of places in the United States.

Centering Climate Adaptation

Climate change will affect cities and districts in ways they haven't imagined and at intensities far greater than they probably have planned for. A decade ago, seasonal wildfire smoke was not an issue to mitigate. The intensity of cloudbursts and flooding is increasing at almost unbelievable rates. The sealing of surfaces in TOD is incredibly high compared with ecodistricts, in part due to the prioritization of automobiles over people, makes them much more vulnerable to intense heat and rain events. Yet climate adaptive planning in TOD is rarely incorporated to the degree it needs to be.

In the context of the 1980s and 1990s, as suburban sprawl was starting to hit the physical limits of continual expansion, TOD may have been an adequate approach. Adding moderate- to high-density neighborhoods near transit is a genuinely smart policy that has taken years of work to overcome a status quo resistant to change. The Institute for Transportation & Development Policy states that TOD is "a critical solution to the unsustainable, car-dependent, and transit-poor urban sprawl that has characterized the growth of cities around the world over the last century. It also contrasts with transit-adjacent development that fails to foster the strong walking and cycling environment needed to complement and actively support the use of public transit."[11] Both transit-adjacent and transit-oriented development *should* be those things! However, in looking at TOD today, through the lens of the polycrisis, it becomes rather clear that the planning of TOD needs a swift and substantial update.

How cities develop will play a major role in whether or not climate goals can be met, with the Intergovernmental Panel on Climate Change Working Group III report noting, "for rapidly growing and emerging urban areas, there is the opportunity to avoid carbon lock-in by focusing on urban form that promotes low-carbon infrastructure and enables low-impact behaviour facilitated by co-located medium to high densities of jobs and housing, walkability, and transit-oriented development."[12] Carbon lock-in occurs when "long-lived, energy and carbon-intensive assets persist, often for decades, and lock out more efficient, lower-carbon alternatives."[13] The path TOD is on in the United States will lock in much more carbon emissions that it should. Ecodistricts offer an opportunity to reverse this unsustainable trend by incorporating dense, climate adaptive neighborhoods with low-carbon technologies where getting groceries or taking the kids to school doesn't require a car, even for larger families.

Seattle's urban planning limits development to as little as a block, or even half a block, off an arterial and immediately falls to detached houses. Not only does this drastically reduce housing options, but it also reduces walkability by focusing it on less enjoyable streets. This is a stark contrast to many European cities, where midrise density exists several blocks off main roads. (Credit: Michael Eliason)

PART I

Planning the Ecodistrict

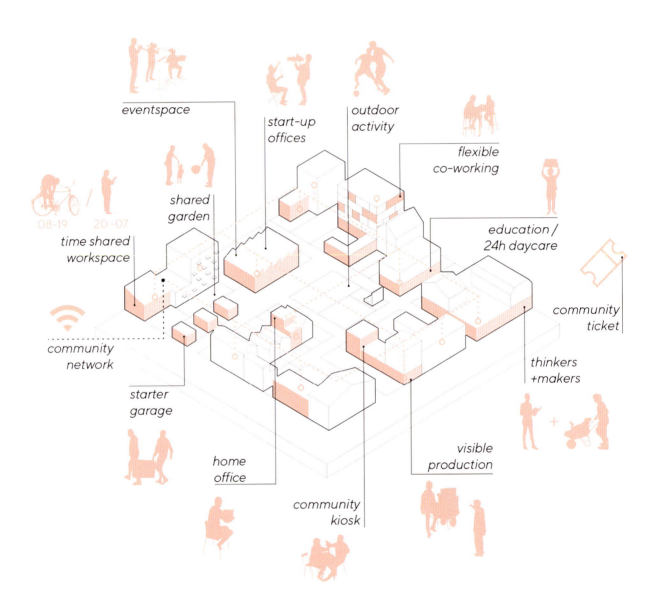

CHAPTER 3

The Productive District

Transitioning away from the monofunctional district, one that is primarily residential or commercial, to a productive mixed-use district with diverse functions is central to the success of car-light and low-carbon ecodistricts. Production in the district can also be used as a means of balancing energy flows for processes to achieve fossil-fuel-free and net zero energy buildings and districts (addressed in Chapter 4).

Manufacturing and production used to be present in the center of the city, and most of the areas currently zoned exclusively for industrial uses in US cities at one point allowed housing and other uses. Intensive mixing of residential and light or nonpolluting industrial uses can be a means of regenerating neighborhoods or districts. The productive city is related to the living milieu, to garage culture, and to vertical urban factories. It is an opportunity to introduce urbanity to existing or obsolete industrial areas. Importantly, as seen in places like Brussels, cities can support productive spaces through innovative leasing, mixed use zoning and microzoning, and prioritization of industry in mixed and residential areas. The productive city can also support a mix of social classes by bringing blue-collar jobs into the city and neighborhoods,[1] in contrast to the economic segregation that is increasingly becoming the norm.

This mixing of uses can take place at the district and even building scale, with hybridized buildings mixing housing and production. There are also opportunities for alternative forms of living, including affordable cluster apartments, workforce housing, and worker cooperatives. The close proximity of residential and light manufacturing does not have to be oppositional; rather, compatible uses can allow for synergies where residents are willing to put up with productive processes and possible noise or other urban nuisances, in exchange for benefits such as free heating, energy production, or large rooftop amenity spaces.

Production can include energy, food and food processes, recycling centers, urban agriculture, and small-scale craft production. Advances in manufacturing

The productive city includes space for a variety of types of production and employment, coexisting with other uses such as dwellings. Even at the block scale, there is ample opportunity for mixing uses and proximity. (Credit: Marc Rieser)

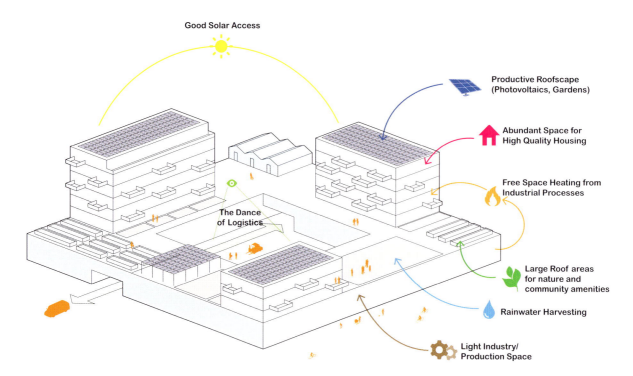

technology (also known as Industry 4.0) have made small-scale manufacturing possible for more people and resulted in a process that is less intrusive, making it easier to mix uses. It is a process that allows for quieter production, less intensive and less polluting production, the incorporation of robotics, and value-added or additive manufacturing. Industry 4.0 could allow industrial and residential uses, which were historically completely incompatible, to have a multitude of synergies while ensuring compatibility in urban districts. According to McKinsey, Industry 4.0 is "the current era of connectivity, advanced analytics, automation, and advanced manufacturing technology that has been transforming global business for years. This wave of change in the manufacturing sector began in the mid-2010s and holds significant potential for operations and the future of production."[2]

The Productive City as Policy Tool

The European Union recognizes that industry and manufacturing are drivers of innovation, research, and productivity—and are largely co-located in metropolitan areas. At the city level, the New Leipzig Charter incorporates the concept of the productive city in order to meet climate goals and prioritize just and sustainable urban development, stating,

> The transformative power of cities is based on a diversified economy which provides jobs while ensuring a sound financial base for sustainable urban development. Cities as attractive, innovative and

The productive city not only brings production back into the city but also allows interesting synergies to coexist between housing and production, such as free heating for residents, ample space for roof gardens, and diverse housing types. (Credit: Michael Eliason/Larch Lab)

24 Building for People

competitive business locations need a skilled workforce, social, technical and logistical infrastructure as well as affordable and accessible space. Ensuring these preconditions, including a favourable innovative environment as well as opportunities for local and regional production should be integral to urban planning.[3]

Vienna has formally adopted the Produktive Stadt (productive city) in its 2025 Stadtentwicklungsplanung (Urban Development Plan).[4] The city views the integration and mixing of industry and housing as necessary for the long-term success of Vienna and attempts to foster new forms of mixing for more sustainable urban development. The city has also been a frontrunner on vertical factories, co-locating several different manufacturing processes in one structure, such as woodmaking, pharmaceuticals, or food production. These can be incorporated in numerous low-rise and midrise facilities being built around the city.[5]

Brussels has adopted the concept of the productive city in its spatial planning and urban governance policies. Brussels chief architect Kristiaan Borret states,

> It isn't about bringing the steel industry back to the city centre. We should also avoid the romantic fantasy of a return of preindustrial crafts. We are in the century of the "Millennials", and creative industries are highly fashionable. From artisanal fabrication of jewelry to bicycle design, fablabs and even micro-breweries, this type of industry is certainly welcome in town, but there are others too. There has to be room for ordinary occupations, such as repair and renovation companies, materials suppliers and the proverbial plumber. There will always be a need for plumbers in the city![6]

The concept, according to Borret, is that as cities redevelop postindustrial brownfields, there are spaces for housing, spaces for jobs, and spaces for the "productive economy, manufacturing, maintenance and repair jobs, food supply . . . being pushed out of the city."[7] The city has spent years researching and implementing the concept and is a frontrunner on new hybrid typologies.

Vertical and Flatted Factories

In many US cities, planning departments have resisted allowing different uses on industrial lands or even maker spaces in residential or commercial areas. Cities are recognizing that these are beneficial, and projects are slowly starting to sprout, such as the NewLab at Brooklyn's Navy Yard, a co-working space for makers.[8] Many cities also have a shortage of industrial space, with industrial lands being hemmed in by housing, offices, or geography. One approach to solving this problem is to intensify industrial lands with multistory projects such as flatted factories. These solutions are not new, and in fact vertical factories have been around for a hundred years. However, many land use codes are not designed to allow innovation or intensification in these areas, leaving a lot of competition for little land, which can ironically lead to gentrification in industrial lands. Cities such as Seattle are trying to get ahead of this and to stem the tide of creeping sprawl of self-storage, with revisions to its comprehensive plans allowing taller and more intensive technology hubs and flatted factories on industrial lands.[9]

Flatted factories are multistory factories or light industrial buildings. They typically share cargo elevators and allow numerous manufacturers to be located in midrise and even high-rise buildings. They are very common in dense cities such as Hong Kong and Singapore and can be leased or bought like a condo. According to the City of London, maker spaces have "an impact not only on their sector but also on local communities. They rely on local suppliers, work with or for people in the area, are involved in training, apprenticeships and job creation. Some workshops have memberships or affiliations in the thousands and have fostered numerous businesses."[10]

One approach to dealing with the shortage of industrial lands is to allow light manufacturing to occur outside land zoned for industry. In 2014, the six-story York Street Industrial Building opened in Portland, Oregon. It was the first vertical factory built in Portland in more than sixty years. The project accommodates dozens of small tenants, and the leasable area is flexible. The project has a number of small-scale producers in the building, including brewers and furniture makers, and logistics is handled through a combination of elevators for people and elevators for moving freight.[11]

Urban production is especially reliant on sustainable logistics to reduce its carbon footprint. Last mile delivery is increasingly vital, and solutions toward e-mobility and carless delivery are necessary to achieve sustainability goals. This will also require rethinking delivery systems, distribution hubs, and other approaches to facilitate the interaction between trucks and cargo bikes or, as noted in Chapter 8, other urban-friendly e-logistics.[12]

There are also opportunities for logistics to become a spectacle where people can watch processes and movement of goods play out, to highlight the inflows and outflows of production. It is also an opportunity to experiment and prioritize sustainable forms of logistics while keeping large freight vehicles out of the pedestrian-friendly core of the district.

In Tokyo, the juxtaposition of production, logistics, housing, and retail all colliding on compact people-oriented streets is incredible. (Credit: Michael Eliason)

The Productive District 27

The Agriquarter

In 2021, I joined a team for the IBA's competition for a new productive district in the city of Winnenden, near Stuttgart. A key member of the team, Julio De la Fuente, is a partner at Gutierrez de la Fuente in Madrid and an expert on the productive city; he had been on the technical committee for the Europan 14 and 15 competitions covering the topic. He has an incredible wealth of knowledge on the topic, and in just a few weeks, we got a crash course on the productive city. Today, I see opportunities for it everywhere.

Winnenden's competition brief was for a mixed-use productive agriculture-focused neighborhood at the outskirts of the city. The city was looking for

Vertical farming may be a more effective conversion than residential for vacant office buildings with deep floor plates. (Credit: Michael Eliason)

new building types combining housing, spaces for growing and food production, and traditional commerce. It was also searching for innovative mobility concepts allowing the neighborhood to be largely car-free. The concepts needed to be experimental, adaptable, and innovative, with an abundance of diverse housing.

The winning entry by JOTT architecture and urbanism incorporates a wild mix of uses on its 14-acre site, including industrial spaces, spaces for start-ups, co-working offices, daycare, mobility hubs, and cafés. Rooftops are also productive and incorporate space for urban agriculture with greenhouses and roof gardens. The core of the district is car-free, allowing for a lively and safe environment for residents. Diverse housing is integrated into each block, allowing new types and mixes to be developed. The total floor area ratio of the district is about 1.85, and the district's framework development plan is moving forward as the district starts to take shape.[13]

Urban agriculture can reduce transportation emissions, placing producers closer to consumers, and even contribute to the circular economy. Vienna is an urban farming hotspot; a third of the tomatoes sold in Austria and over 60 percent of eggplants and cucumbers are grown there.[14] Hut & Stiehl is a company in Vienna growing oyster mushrooms in soil composed of used coffee grounds from the city's numerous coffee shops. The mushrooms are delivered by e-bike, and the coffee grounds can be composted into new soil afterwards.[15] In Japan, several cities are seeing a growth in vertical farming, largely in existing buildings with growing vacancies, owing in part to demographic shifts from increasingly depopulated rural areas and an aging population.[16]

Productive cities mark a return to the way cities developed centuries ago but with significantly less pollution and fewer safety hazards. It is possible to create pleasant environments with compatible functions.

The productive district offers numerous benefits to cities, to workers, and to neighborhoods. It offers the opportunity to increase quality of life through reduced commute times, traffic, and pollution. It increases the tax base and allows for quick exchange of information and chance encounters. It can also give identity to place. Having affordable spaces for incubators and startups is necessary, as is support from the local manufacturing sector, technology, and institutional actors such as universities and schools. As cities start to think about the circular economy and how its loops are integrated, the productive district will become a key component.

CHAPTER 4

Net Zero and Fossil-Fuel-Free Districts

In 2013, a mass timber office building called the Bullitt Center opened in Seattle. It was designed to meet the requirements of the Living Building Challenge, one of the world's most rigorous sustainable building standards. One of its most recognizable features is a massive photovoltaic (PV) canopy projecting out over the public right of way. It was an ambitious project, and a decade in, it is producing 30 percent more energy than it consumes.[1] The Bullitt Center was one of the first office buildings in the world to be net zero energy, which means that it produces as least as much energy as it consumes. It is notable for catching up the US construction industry to that of the European Union and reframing our thinking on how energy efficiency and energy production can be complementary.

Net zero energy commercial and multifamily buildings have been feasible for years, but the Bullitt Center was the first notable midrise project in the United States to hit that mark. Since it was completed, the cost of PV installations has decreased dramatically,[2] and better energy efficiency measures have also become easier or even mandated. Passive House, the ultra-low-energy building standard discussed in Chapter 16, pairs extremely well with net zero buildings, making it easier to move away from fossil fuel reliance and reducing the energy needed to heat, cool, ventilate, and operate a building. Even in urban settings, it can be possible to offset energy production with rooftop PVs, although it can create a conflict for urban buildings because it can limit rooftop access as an amenity. An intriguing solution to accommodate both rooftop PV and roof decks has been used numerous times by the Philadelphia-based firm Onion Flats Architecture. They create a canopy that the PV sits on top of, allowing the roof to still be used as an amenity. A pleasant benefit to this is additional shade from the sun that roof decks typically do not have.

Frankfurt's Aktiv-Stadthaus is an incredible 525-foot-long by 30-foot-deep social housing project that was completed in 2015. Part of the façade and the roof of the eight-story project are covered with PVs. The project uses

In Philadelphia, Onion Flats Architecture have created a productive roofscape with space for biodiversity, with photovoltaics situated above a green roof system. This can be viewed from an adjacent rooftop amenity space. (Credit: Onion Flats Architecture and GRASS Green Roofs and Solar Systems)

incredibly efficient appliances and is effectively a Passive House, driving down the energy demand. Heat is supplied largely by a heat exchanger running through adjacent sewer lines. Aktiv-Stadthaus was the first multifamily project in in the heart of a German city to produce more energy in a year than it consumed, even accounting for the building's electric carshare.[3] On an annual basis, Frankfurt receives as much insolation as Nome, Alaska. If energy-positive multifamily midrise buildings, producing more energy than they are consuming, are possible in Germany, they are possible anywhere in the United States and most of Canada.

Net Zero Buildings → Net Zero Districts

Bahnstadt (Train City) is Heidelberg's 287-acre Passive House district located on the outskirts of its historic core. Though not quite net zero, the low-energy district is an example of how to achieve net zero communities at the urban scale. The mixed-use district is designed for up to 6,800 residents, with space for up to 6,000 workstations. Half of the residents of the district are under thirty years old, and the compact walkable and bike-friendly district is attractive for families. Children under eighteen years old are 20 percent of the district's population, which has eight daycare facilities and a primary school.[4] The buildings in Bahnstadt were required to meet the Passive House standard, and use the city's district heating system to provide space heating and domestic hot water. According to a Passive House Institute's monitoring report, the space heating requirement for buildings in the district is nearly 90 percent lower than for existing buildings connected to the system. The total consumption including plug loads came in at 55 kWh/m^2, proving that low-energy districts are feasible.[5]

When building loads are small enough, through meeting a demanding standard such as Passive House or the Living Building Challenge, it is feasible to add PVs to produce enough energy to offset the energy consumed by the building. This means that zero energy districts are feasible with today's technology. In Ann Arbor, Michigan, THRIVE Collaborative's 13.59-acre Veridian at County Farm features 160 homes, from detached houses to affordable apartment buildings, where rooftop PVs will offset all energy consumed on site, making it one of the first net zero energy districts in the United States.

Fossil Gas Exit

Fossil gas heavily contributes to global warming, is toxic, and with today's technology is no longer needed for cooking or heating. *Fossil gas* is a term climate advocates and I use for "natural gas" in order to better highlight its toxic and environmentally destructive nature. A 2021 study noted that largely because of the usage of the term *natural gas* instead of *fossil gas* or *methane gas*, the public perceives it to be less environmentally destructive than it is.[6]

Induction cooktops offer fast, highly controlled cooking without any of the toxicity of fossil gas cooktops and ovens. (Credit: Lora Teagarden)

As an architect, I have not always won the argument on switching to induction, because clients gave in to the marketing of gas stoves by fossil gas companies. Even when discussing the health benefits of forgoing fossil gas for cooking and heating, many still wanted fossil gas stoves, thanks to decades of industry marketing.[7] Research is rapidly changing minds on this, however, and industry offerings for electric appliances and mechanical equipment have increased dramatically. Several US cities have also passed laws against fossil gas hookups in new construction. When you cook with fossil gas, the byproducts of combustion include carbon monoxide and nitrogen dioxide, and the health effects of both are quite serious.[8] A study on the effects of indoor gas stoves found that 13 percent of childhood asthma cases in the United States were due to them.[9] Thanks to the speed and efficiency of induction cooktops, those dangers may be limited. Notable chefs such as Eric Ripert[10] and J. Kenji López-Alt[11] have advocated the benefits of induction cooking, such as better control and better speed. Also, it doesn't poison your friends and family—seems like an easy switch.

Reliability has long been argued as a main reason for keeping fossil gas in buildings. However, the extreme weather events associated with climate

Net Zero and Fossil-Fuel-Free Districts 33

change provide evidence to the contrary. In 2023, the Federal Energy Regulatory Commission released a report highlighting the lack of reliability of fossil gas for powering the grid after Winter Storm Elliott,[12] which hit just a year after Winter Storm Uri led to the death of at least 250 people.[13]

It turns out that fossil gas is unreliable when energy is needed most. Also, it can build up in homes, leading to explosions resulting in extensive damage and death. The time to move beyond fossil gas has arrived.

Electrify Everything

With modern energy codes and heat pumps, there's no need to use fossil gas for space heating or even domestic hot water. In Bayern, the new low-energy

Domestic hot water is one of the last areas in the construction sector to see widespread electrification. This is rapidly changing with options such as the WaterDrop, a prefabricated drop-in domestic hot water system for large multifamily buildings, using SANCO's low–global warming potential refrigerant heat pumps and insulated storage tanks. (Credit: Small Planet Supply)

fourplex we lived in used an air source heat pump for both hot water and space heating with radiant flooring. With the passage of the Inflation Reduction Act and increasingly stringent energy codes, there are growing incentives and product offerings for space heating and domestic hot water. One of those options is Small Planet Supply's SANCO CO_2 WaterDrop, a packaged drop-in heat pump hot water system for multifamily and commercial buildings that is the first available in the United States to incorporate CO_2 as a low-carbon refrigerant.[14] Many heat pumps can also provide cooling. Heat pumps are incredibly efficient, and they aren't limited to just cool and mild climates. Heat pumps can operate at temperatures well below freezing, and according to Jan Rosenow and colleagues,[15] over 60 percent of households in Norway and over 40 percent in Finland and Sweden use heat pumps.

Passive Houses. Heat pumps. Active solar protection to reduce cooling needs. Photovoltaics. Sewer heat exchangers. Batteries. Waste heat recovery. District heating and cooling. Fossil-fuel-free and zero energy ecodistricts are already a possibility and should be prioritized for public health reasons alone. European cities have been using energy modeling to minimize urban heat islands and maximize energy production for years. The next decade will be incredible as positive energy districts, producing more energy than they consume—even accounting for electric mobility—are already in planning.[16] The district scale is also beneficial for balancing energy through load shifting and storage. As the European Union scales up to 100 net zero cities by 2030, there are several research projects studying this issue, including three mixed-use positive energy districts in Austria.[17]

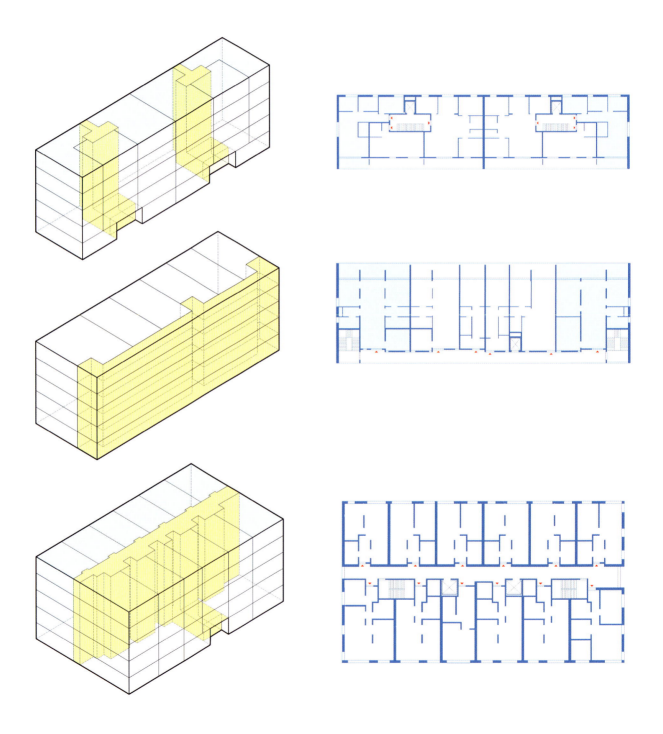

36 Building for People

CHAPTER 5

Unlocking Ecodistricts with Better Regulations

In December 2018, Architekturbüro Leinhäupl + Neuber, the firm I worked for, won an architecture competition for a twelve-story pencil-thin mixed-use tower in Augsburg, Germany. I sat there looking at the drawings, closely studying the floorplans, and just could not figure out what was missing. Then it hit me. This proposal had only one stairway, with associated elevators. When I asked my boss why it didn't have two sets of stairways, as would be required in the United States, he looked at me and said, "Sorry, I do not understand. Would this small project require two stairs in America?" Indeed, it would! It would have two stairways, plus an elevator core, plus the circulation connecting them all, which would have consumed over half of the typical floor and probably rendered this project infeasible because the small footprint could not have accommodated a second stair and met the programmatic requirements.

This is where my journey in understanding how abnormally we plan our housing in the United States began, a journey shaped by researching foreign housing patterns and regulations while working abroad.

Living and working in Seattle proved to be fortuitous on the topic of what I call point access blocks: compact buildings with homes arranged around a single central stair and elevator core. Seattle has allowed point access blocks for nearly fifty years, when the council adopted changes allowing taller single-stair buildings in 1977. They were originally allowed with no height limit and conditions to ensure a high level of safety, including a maximum of four dwellings per floor and fire-rated assemblies. In the 1980s, there were a series of downzones across the city, and the height limit for point access blocks was reduced to six stories. That six-story limit still exists today, although there are numerous conditions to ensure these buildings are safe: a maximum travel distance, fire-rated assemblies, a maximum number of dwellings per floor per stair (still four!), and of course fire sprinklers. In a twist of fate, when I arrived back in Seattle during the COVID lockdown, one of the projects I worked on was a small five-story point access block apartment building.

Unit access plays a significant role in the livability and climate adaptation of a building. There are three main ways to access a unit: point access blocks (top), single-loaded corridors (middle), and double-loaded corridors (bottom). Note the shallower building depth for point access blocks and single-loaded corridors. (Credit: Michael Eliason/Larch Lab)

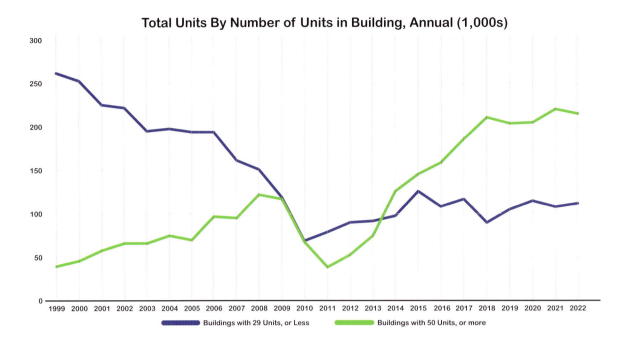

After writing and talking about this issue for several years, I was hired by the City of Vancouver in 2019 to write a report on point access blocks, which launched the formation of Larch Lab as an architecture and urbanism studio and a policy-oriented "think and do" tank. From there, the media interest has steadily increased, and an educational campaign has grown into a national movement. This is what prompted Larch Lab to prepare a policy brief for cities, politicians, and housing activists to better understand the differences in unit access and building codes. I helped write Washington State's Point Access Block bill, which was unanimously adopted into law in 2023, and have been collaborating with a larger network on potential legislation in other states. To date, point access block legislation has passed in California; Oregon; Virginia; Nashville, Tennessee; and Washington. Minnesota, New York State, and Colorado have all had point access block bills introduced.[1] Thanks to Seattle's taller point access block regulations, there are some incredible projects with family-sized dwellings that have been completed in the last decade, as architects become aware of the possibilities.

Unit Access Is Everything

New development in the United States has been trending toward significantly larger buildings over the last few decades. According to the US Census Bureau, multifamily buildings with fifty or more dwellings made up just 13 percent of all multifamily homes in 2000. By 2020, that number had quadrupled to 55 percent of all multifamily homes.[2] This trend toward larger buildings is not great from an urban planning standpoint, and even *The New York Times*

The number of large apartment buildings with fifty or more units in the United States has been steadily increasing over the last twenty-five years. Smaller buildings, which used to be more prevalent, have become quite rare. This is in part a function of our building codes, cities drastically increasing floor area ratio on a few sites instead of distributing it broadly, and development financing. (Data source: US Census Bureau)

has weighed in on the banality of these massive buildings.[3] These buildings tend to be much more capital intensive. The building code for multiple stairways requires parcel assemblage in previously developed areas, because the small footprints of existing buildings on small lots would not be economically feasible with multiple stairways. This increases the cost of land for development, complexity of projects, and associated development timelines and risks. Enabling smaller-scale developments such as missing middle and midrise housing increases opportunities for small property owners, small developers, community land trusts, cooperatives, and even homeowners—organizations that are not typically able to deliver massive, highly capitalized projects—to meet today's housing needs. This is increasingly important, because the housing crisis in the United States today is broad and growing and is no longer confined to just a handful of cities on the coasts.[4]

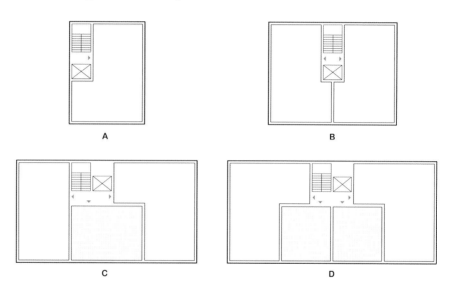

The majority of multifamily development in the United States and Canada is in large, hotel-like buildings called double-loaded corridors. These are buildings with a hallway down the middle and dwellings flanking either side. Perhaps you are envisioning scenes from Stephen King's *The Shining*: long, dark, creepy, anonymous hallways with no daylight. This central corridor connects dwellings on a floor with two (or sometimes more) exit stairways. This building is almost nonexistent in European countries, with exceptions for assisted living facilities and student dormitories.

In German, a point access block is called a Spaenner. These are typically found in configurations of one to four units positioned around a central core with a single stair and elevator. (Credit: Michael Eliason/Larch Lab)

There are numerous problems with double-loaded corridor buildings. Apartments situated on highways or arterials have little respite from noise pollution. Those homes also may see more exposure to dust and grime from air pollution and tires. With increased warming due to climate change, there are almost no dwellings that are able to cross-ventilate or night purge to

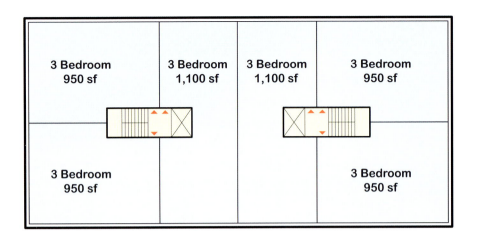

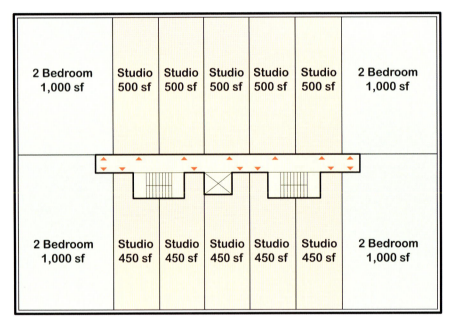

reduce overheating. For children and older adults, the anonymity of long corridors can make wayfinding incredibly challenging. Because of the economics of construction, it is often difficult to get larger dwellings to work, as three- and four-bedroom dwellings would be competing against the rent from three or four separate studios. These buildings also tend to be thicker and bulkier than others, reducing space for trees, nature, gathering, or climate adaptation.

Point Access Blocks: The Workhorse of Urban Housing

US building codes severely constrain the use of the workhorse of urban housing found the world over: point access blocks. As mentioned, a point access block is a compact building with dwellings arranged around a single central

Diagram comparing the depth of a point access block (top) with a double-loaded corridor building (bottom). These buildings have the same number of bedrooms; however, the point access block requires just two thirds the floor area, two thirds the number of bathrooms, and less than half the number of kitchens. (Credit: Michael Eliason/Larch Lab)

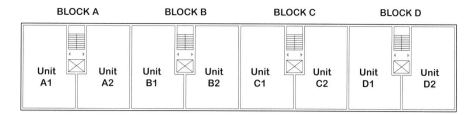
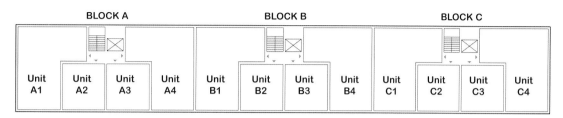

In countries where taller point access blocks are allowed, large development is still common, but instead of double-loaded corridors, several point access blocks are ganged together in series. This allows for more livable and climate adaptive homes in structures that have a smaller and more community-oriented scale and feel. (Credit: Michael Eliason/Larch Lab)

stair and elevator core. These types of buildings are found throughout Asian, South American, and European cities. Though rare, they can also be found in the United States in Seattle, New York City, and Oahu. They are also found across a spectrum of place types: rural villages, suburbs, small urban infill sites, and even vast estates where several point access blocks can be connected to form larger buildings. They can unlock smaller missing middle and midrise development sites, specifically at the level of development between missing middle housing and highrises. The benefits of point access blocks are numerous; they are the superfruit of ecodistricts. They offer the potential to unlock more affordable housing through more compact but livable homes (e.g., 800 square feet for a two bedroom instead of 1,000 square feet, which may be more typical in the United States) and significantly smaller buildings. They offer more family-friendly housing through larger and more livable dwellings, and more dwellings that are accessible or adaptable as midrise buildings require elevators, whereas low-rise ones do not.[5]

Perhaps the most important benefit is that they result in a better unit mix, with larger and more family-sized homes. Point access blocks achieve this in two ways: through the reduced floor area of the redundant stairway and connecting corridor and through limitations on the number of dwellings per stair, which induces development to fill the building envelope with larger homes. With the postpandemic increase in work from home, larger dwellings and ones with either more bedrooms or spaces that can be used as home offices are probably going to see higher demand. This is the most cost-effective method I have found to deliver these sorts of homes.

Perhaps most importantly, point access blocks allow for more climate adaptive homes that can cross-ventilate, a necessity for the extreme urban heat we are seeing with global warming.

Thinner buildings allow for daylight on two or even three sides of a home. Although daylight can be found in older housing in places such as New York City and Boston, because of the corridor running through the middle of US multifamily housing, it is challenging to find new apartments with daylight on multiple sides. Bedrooms in point access blocks can be positioned on the quiet side of the building, allowing for better sleeping environments.

Nearly all of Europe, with the exception of Ireland, allows point access blocks to at least five stories, and most allow them to be significantly taller. In 2023, the UK government announced a reduction in point access blocks from having no height limit to 18 meters (59 feet), or seven stories—fully four stories taller than most US building regulations currently allow.[6] Although the 2017 Grenfell Tower fire in London was cited as a reason for this change, the Grenfell report does not state that single-stair buildings were at fault. Germany allows single-stair residential and even office buildings up to 60 meters (197 feet) with certain requirements, including pressurized stairways to evacuate smoke buildup, fire-rated assemblies, and smoke-proof doors. Switzerland has no height limit for single-stair buildings, and they also have some of the world's lowest building fire death rates. Unlike the United States, nearly all European countries, including Switzerland with no height limit, do not even require sprinklers for the majority of midrise or high-rise housing.[7]

Point access blocks are legal under the International Building Code (the model building code in the United States) but limited to only three stories.

Typical floor plan for Larix, a proposed six-story Passive House and mass timber Baugruppe in Seattle with two connected point access blocks, allowing for family-sized homes, units that cross-ventilate, and bedrooms positioned on the quiet side of the building. (Credit: Michael Eliason/ Larch Lab)

42 Building for People

Oahu and the cities of Seattle and New York have exceptions allowing up to six stories. Vermont allows up to four stories. In Canada, point access blocks are restricted to just two floors. Conrad Speckert, whose McGill University master of architecture thesis was on point access blocks,[8] has worked with a task force in Canada to propose a code modification to allow six-story point access blocks nationwide. British Columbia's housing minister announced at the end of 2023 that the BC government would be expediting adoption of point access blocks and may pursue a path to allow eight-story buildings.

Thinking Thin

Another peculiarity for much of America is that we do not regulate building depth to the degree found elsewhere. When I was working in Germany, both building depth and form were heavily regulated. Daylighting and quality of life are considerations for many other countries, with building codes requiring minimum daylighting levels or access to natural light and ventilation. Most

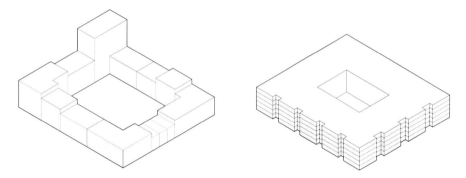

At the scale of the urban block, point access blocks (left) can allow for more diversity in building height, as well as architecture with several different buildings on one block face. Double-loaded corridors (right) lack this diversity, so planners play games to break up the façade with different building materials or modulation to make it appear smaller. Note the larger courtyard in the point access block. (Credit: Michael Eliason/Larch Lab)

European development is limited to about 35 to 60 feet in depth. As building floor plates have trended deeper in the United States and buildings are significantly bulkier, cities have moved toward adopting requirements such as façade modulation—changes in façade planes—or material changes in order to make these buildings appear less massive. Of course, these games do little to break up the massing. However, they do result in a number of problems from an economic and environmental standpoint. More reentrant corners from the undulating façade increase exterior surface area and the amount of materials used in the façade. These planning moves result in higher embodied carbon emissions, higher construction costs, increased maintenance risks, and more energy consumed to heat and cool the building (which results in even higher carbon emissions).

In Seattle, new buildings tend to be more than 50 percent deeper than typical new construction in Switzerland or Germany—roughly 80 feet deep versus 50 feet deep. This depth puts apartments on the courtyard side of the buildings significantly closer together, reducing privacy and access to daylight. Unfortunately, the trend appears to be going in the wrong direction in the United States, with recently proposed projects in Los Angeles, Seattle, and Denver having floor plates exceeding the 100-foot depth mark. The apartments in these buildings will be incredibly deep single-aspect dwellings with windows

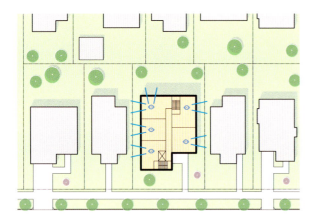 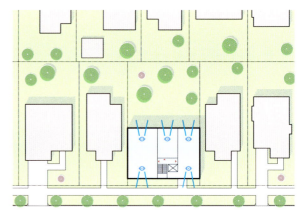

on only one side, often with one and sometimes even two windowless bedrooms. Failing to constrain these extreme depths will lead to more housing that is unable to adapt to a changing climate, with no ability to mitigate or adapt to extreme heat, either through cross-ventilation, night purging, or abundant space for trees.

By contrast, buildings in European ecodistricts tend to be narrow, but taller, or at least, narrower with the flexibility for going taller on accent buildings or inducing more tenure diversity. Thinner buildings are the key to unlocking more open space for uses such as stormwater mitigation, blue-green infrastructure, socializing, play, and, perhaps most importantly in a warming world, space for trees to mitigate urban heat islands.

This isn't to say that point access block development is all that should be allowed, but planners and politicians should be thinking about the effects climate will have on buildings and on the physical and mental health of those living and working in them.

There are still possibilities to achieve very livable double-loaded corridor buildings at the 60-foot limit, and single-loaded corridors—buildings with dwellings situated only on one side of an internal or external corridor, set to the building perimeter—work quite well within this depth, including homes that allow daylight on opposing sides and cross-ventilation.

In the United States, infill and small-scale urban development tends to be oriented to neighboring lots (left), with deep buildings leaving little room for trees, green space, or blue-green infrastructure. Positioning infill closer to the street with point access blocks (right) allows homes to be oriented with more eyes on the street or a rear courtyard while allowing abundant space for nature and blue-green infrastructure in the same building footprint. (Credit: Michael Eliason/Larch Lab)

44 Building for People

Enabling Small-Scale Urban Development

In the last decade, there have been dozens of projects in Seattle, each with more than 200 homes. This isn't the case in countries such as the Netherlands and Germany, where small and medium-sized projects still prevail. I have spent countless hours studying floorplans of German multifamily housing and have seen only a handful of recent projects anywhere near that size, with the majority being student housing. New large-scale development in Germany is often broken up into multiple lots with smaller, separate buildings, creating the possibility of derisking projects while ensuring they aren't of a vastly different scale than what is already present.

It is this combination of point access blocks and thin buildings that allows development to achieve the fine-grained urbanism found in both old and new European ecodistricts and settlements. In Heilbronn, Germany's Neckarbogen district, blocks are broken up into smaller parcels of seven to ten buildings, all of them point access blocks. The courtyards of these blocks are larger than those we tend to find in large US cities. The diversity in buildings at the block level induces aesthetic variety without façades designed to create the illusion that they aren't massive. It also allows for a wider variety of housing types and tenures: market-rate housing, social housing, Baugruppen,

An aerial of Heilbronn's Neckarbogen district showing how small-scale urban development is facilitated with point access blocks even in modern development. Each of these buildings looks different, because they are in both design and tenure: workforce housing, market-rate housing, Baugruppen, and social housing. (Credit: WÖHR Autoparksysteme GmbH)

Unlocking Ecodistricts with Better Regulations   45

and workforce housing. It is this fine-grained nature that enables a better economic and social mix of residents. Compare this with new development in the United States, where an entire city block is one or two separate developments. There is very little affordable housing, most of the dwellings are market rate. Perhaps a handful of token affordable homes are required for the right to develop the project. Until our codes are updated to allow this combination that results in more diversity at the block level, much as historical development patterns used to allow, US cities will struggle to break away from an incredibly unaffordable and monotonous status quo.

CHAPTER 6

Planning the Ecodistrict

Vienna's Seestadt Aspern is the result of an international urban planning competition with public dialogue. Planning competitions typically result in higher-quality places. (Credit: Lukasz Karnas)

The planning and design process of urban district development in Europe frontloads public participation and community input, as opposed to gathering it throughout the process, as is typical in the United States. The outcomes could not be more disparate. Planning and community input processes in the United States have been broken for decades, and this is especially noticeable to anyone attending a planning meeting in the United States today.[1] Part of the

problem stems from project procurement. In the United States, most urban planning or master planning projects will be awarded based on a request for proposals (RFP). An RFP is issued when the scope is known, with a selection process that looks at planning team fees and design approach.

The RFP process is rather archaic, and although it may not be intentional, it keeps younger and more diverse firms from winning projects and stifles innovation.[2] It is difficult for young firms to land public projects, because the selection criteria are based largely on proposed fees and similar experience. Established firms, with lower fees, that routinely hit their project budgets (albeit with the banal, placeless landscapes and buildings found in Anywhere, USA) thrive on the RFP process. It also isn't typically a blind evaluation process—proposals include résumés and headshots—so additional barriers and biases can evolve through the selection and interview process, which as noted in the *Harvard Business Review* can lead to "suboptimal decision making."[3]

An RFP could be written to remove some of the inherent biases in the selection process, but this is rare. RFPs are typically scored on a team's knowledge, design approach, experience, fees, and timeline. Participation by minority- or woman-owned enterprises may not even be mandated or evaluated. These are not processes for ensuring high-quality, equitable, or innovative outcomes.

In China and most European countries, the procurement process for public and sometimes even private works is through design competitions. In the European Union, these are mandated for commissions above a certain value.[4] These are juried competitions, which are an effective way to increase design quality over other procurement methods, although this process is also far from perfect. Traditionally, design competitions have been completely anonymous, removing a large part of bias on the side of the jurors.

A joint declaration by the International Union of Architects and the Architects Council of Europe highlights the numerous benefits of design competitions, including "quality, innovation, transparency, flexibility, guarantee of quality, cost-efficiency, the opportunity for public participation, equal opportunity, and creativity."[5] As in the RFP process, there is the potential for exploitation in certain competition formats and the unpaid labor involved in preparing the entry, which is why some architecture organizations and countries are moving toward a model with very low-barrier prequalifications and honoraria for the invited entrants.[6]

Brussels may have one of the better approaches for project procurement via design competitions, for both public and private projects. The competitions

Aerial view of Vienna's 593-acre Seestadt Aspern district, which has a capacity for 25,000 residents and 20,000 jobs. The district features most amenities needed for daily life, including schools and abundant open space. The 5-acre artificial lake plays a role in both stormwater management and evaporative cooling. (Credit: Christian Fürthner)

have a two-stage process, with a low-barrier prequalification to allow access to more firms. The top three to five candidates are invited to submit a proposed design and are paid a stipend for their time. The process is open and transparent, with a professional jury determining the winner. A report on the decisions and process is then published. According to chief architect Kristiaan Borret, the city's approach leads to better outcomes and higher-quality projects while opening up opportunities for younger and new firms—without relying on unpaid labor.[7]

WYSIWYG

The design competition process allows something that the RFP process does not: The jury and public to have an immediate sense of what the proposed project will be like long before the first shovel hits the ground. A sense of the urban character, the quality of the urban space, the mobility connections, the housing mix, the open space—what you see is what you get.

In the United States, the initial design process is significantly longer, with multiple layers of outreach coming after the project has been initiated, and the processes used often include multiple opportunities for public input that become a forum to claw back or water down designs—less housing, more parking, or poorer neighborhood connections.

The design competition takes a different approach, with public participation largely frontloaded on the timeline with residents' needs, wishes, and critiques of the project, as well as necessary information related to local context. Often for urban planning competitions, there are a number of expert talks and citizen workshops to further incorporate strategies, concepts, and best practices into the brief. Online informational and participation events are increasingly the norm. These all help inform the local needs for types of housing; type, quality, and amount of open and green space; desired sustainability and energy production goals; protection of nature; mobility; and architectural character. All of this is collated into a lengthy competition brief, which includes the program: the spatial requirements, targeted number of homes, space for schools or other uses, and amount of open space. It also includes planning goals of the competition: whether the district is car-free, the coordination with transit or future transit, prioritizing people-centered streets and places, the mix of uses, housing and building types, and whether there is a focus on post–fossil fuel energies. The brief also typically includes extensive information on existing conditions, mobility connections, climate plans, nature protection, mapped noise pollution, and sometimes air pollution issues.

The project is judged on a variety of criteria: whether the proposed entry meets the owner's minimum requirements laid out by the brief, the mix of uses and housing types, the open space qualities, the urban form and character,

A rendering of the "Green Loop" in Hamburg's Oberbillwerder district, showing the planned interplay between nature, stormwater management, and urban character. (Credit: By ADEPT and Karres en Brands)

and how development is shaped and phased. Juries are composed largely of industry professionals with relevant experience: urban planners, architects, city planners, and occasionally politicians or other local representatives. As was the case in Cologne's Max Becker Areal, they can also have nonvoting members and subject matter experts specializing in mobility, sustainability, commerce, stormwater management, and air and noise pollution.[8] Projects are scored, winners are announced, prizes are awarded based on rankings, and the overall winner is invited to negotiate the project's framework development plan. At this stage, it isn't an opportunity to water down or delay the project; it is instead a refinement of the competition winner with input from the public and government agencies.

Inducing Urban Innovation

The competition process can also be a method for exploring new forms of urbanism or living. This is the case with Copenhagen's Fælledby district, being built on a green field that was once landfilled. Henning Larsen's

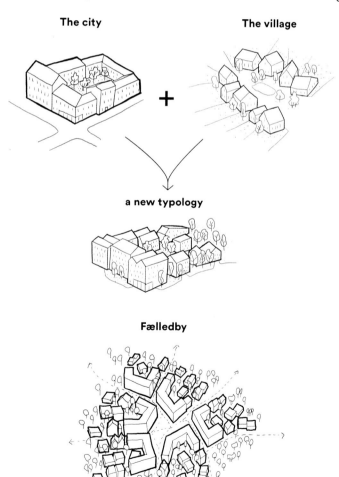

The planning competition allows room for innovation and creativity. In their proposal for the Fælledby district in Copenhagen, Henning Larsen combined aspects of the compact city and villages to develop a new hybrid typology for this interstitial site. (Credit: Henning Larsen)

winning design envisions it as a hybridized space, combining the character of the rural village with a denser urban district to create a new diaphanous space that blends in natural settings where preservation of nature and open space are priorities. The district, planned largely with wood structures, will consist of 2,000 homes, a quarter of which will be social housing. In addition, there will be daycare facilities, a school, grocery stores, restaurants, and cafés. Forty percent of the district's 44 acres will be preserved natural habitats. From the center of the district, residents and visitors can walk to natural landscapes in just a few minutes.[9]

The Rahmenplan (Framework Development Plan) refines the physical characteristics of the district based on the competition design. The plan includes layouts of the various types of streets, from pedestrianized ones to low-volume neighborhood streets and collector streets or arterials, with an eye toward sustainable forms of mobility; the dimensions of open space and connections within and around the district; the qualities of parks and green space; the mix of uses and where they are located in the district. Building heights and numbers of floors are typically indicated as well, as are dimensions of buildings at the block level and how they are parceled. Development of the district ensues, based on these documents. Individual buildings are typically designed by different architecture teams, working with owners (public or private), thus ensuring another level of qualitative differentiation compared with the half- or full-sized block development in the United States.

This rendering shows the varied scale and connection to nature proposed for Fælledby. Competitions allow residents and policymakers to know what the potentialities of a site or district are early in the process. (Credit: Henning Larsen)

Concept Tendering

The United States has not really engaged in city building for decades. US cities often don't have the budget, the capacity, or the appetite to take on development themselves. However, this is exactly the approach that cities can and must take to lead on urban development.

Steingauquartier in Kirchheim unter Teck, just outside Stuttgart, is one of the flagship projects for Stuttgart's International Building Exhibition. The district is a nearly car-free 9-acre parcel developed on what was formerly a shopping mall. The city worked with residents to find out what their needs and wants were, acquired the land, and initiated the development planning and engineering. The city then set about developing the infrastructure and public realm.[10] Because the city owned the land, they set a fixed price to recoup their investment costs for developing the site and infrastructure. This allowed them to incentivize a broad social and economic mix of residents: Baugruppen, attached single-family homes, affordable housing, and luxury housing. The process of awarding the parcels was based on project concepts and quality instead of going to the highest bidder.[11] This process privileges values (e.g., socially inclusive, ecologically friendly [passive house, mass timber] housing) and resulted in buildings for families, multigenerational homes, and places for residents with disabilities or dementia. Sale of land from the various parcels came in slightly higher than the city's own outlay costs. Ground floor activation resulted in a number of community spaces, affordable co-working spaces and ateliers, a bakery, a café, restaurants, even a dentist's office. The courtyards of each block are communally owned and offer a variety of experiences.[12]

As architecture researcher Robert Temel notes, this process, called Konzeptvergabe (concept tendering), is used to reduce monopolization and sterility, increase competition, and allow smaller and more innovative developers or nonmarket actors to provide an array of housing.[13] Concept tendering has its roots in the German city of Tübingen and has spread to Hamburg, Freiburg, Berlin, and even Vienna. Using the lift in value of the land to finance the cost of development is called land value capture. Land value capture is one of the most effective approaches to developing equitable transit-oriented development and ecodistricts, yet it is illegal or infeasible in several states. Tax increment financing is another form of value capture where government can increase property taxes to finance the debts incurred developing infrastructure, which increases property values.

City control of developable land is almost always the optimal path toward more equitable outcomes. As in Kirchheim, Tübingen controlled most of

the land in its district-scale developments, as did Freiburg. Munich-Riem and Vienna's Seestadt Aspern are massive districts built on former airports. Many ecodistricts in Europe are built on the sites of former military bases and barracks. Amsterdam owns 80 percent of the land in the city and uses ground leases to ensure perpetual control of the land, allowing them significant flexibility in how the city adapts and changes.

The good news is there is ample public land in US cities that could be used for ecodistricts, including land owned by the city and its departments, state agencies, government agencies, quasigovernment agencies, and the military. One such path to highlighting how much there is, and where it is, is simply to map it. The Home & Hope Mapping Tool was developed by Enterprise Community Partners, with geographic information system maps used to filter where public and tax-exempt land that could be used for affordable housing in King County is located.[14]

Private land, which is where most transit-oriented development is located, can use these same processes. Private landowners and developers need to

Internal view of a courtyard in Kirchheim unter Teck's Steingauquartier, showing space for play, private outdoor space, and diverse architecture envisioned in the original scheme. (Credit: Gernot Pohl)

work with local government on zoning changes, and this can be where community benefits through increased levels of affordable housing can and should be realized. In France, the Zone d'Amenagement Concrete district development process is led by public agencies, although it may be implemented as a public–private partnership. The Netherlands uses a fascinating public–private process for land readjustment called the Urbanisator, where numerous landowners temporarily transfer their land to a public or private entity that engages in the spatial planning of the district. The landowners then receive land on which to build their projects.[15]

Often in the United States, planning departments are reluctant to look at models that would change the underlying street configuration or infrastructure around transit. Zoning levels are merely increased, allowing increased density but with minimal consideration to public benefit. By failing to transform the area around transit to prioritize better public realms and better block configurations for dense and car-light development, cities are locking in autocentric places unable to adapt to change. An approach where municipalities lead the planning process (but not the design process), that works in tandem with the community and developers for a transformation prioritizing connectedness, affordability, climate adaptation, and high-quality places, could result in better outcomes.

Climate Modeling in Planning

Increasingly, climate modeling is being used to elucidate the interaction of buildings, open space, and the public realm. The Zurich Goldacker Settlement two-stage competition was an opportunity to pilot the use of climate modeling to inform the development of districts and settlements in order to reduce urban heat islands and ensure cooler temperatures for residents. After the first round of their planning competitions, the city showed best- and worst-case scenarios on building and block formations and their effect on the district's ability to cool off. The final four shortlisted entries were modeled to give the jury a sense of the climate outcomes related to designs. The winning entry is a series of tall, diaphanous buildings with abundant green space, numerous trees, and vegetation allowing cool air to permeate the site during summer. The project is currently in planning, and the city views adopting new processes such as this as essential for inducing better climate outcomes and for modeling smarter planning for other cities and developers in the face of climate change.[16]

Cities must find ways to change their spatial planning to adapt to and mitigate the effects of climate change. This is especially true for areas where dense new districts will be built. Cities must also expedite and streamline planning processes. It took less than three years for Hamburg's Senate to authorize Oberbillwerder's engagement and planning process and sign off on the district's masterplan.[17] Similarly, the process from public engagement to masterplan approval in Vienna's Seestadt also took three years. These districts are massive and will take decades to build out. Ensuring a framework that delivers a high level of quality, in a rapid manner—yet remains flexible to changing demands—will be critical to the success of the district.

CHAPTER 7

Community Participation

Civic engagement is critical to the success of the ecodistrict. A top-down approach, where cities or institutions dictate what will happen, leaves citizens unable to participate in decision making. It can lead to a failure to obtain community buy-in. An engaged public can be committed to ensuring the success of a project, and the knowledge of local residents typically far exceeds what a jurisdiction can assemble on their own. The United Nations notes that without an inclusive and collaborative engagement process, planning outcomes are likely to be less fair and benefit the few rather than the public.[1] Inclusive public engagement can also result in "more innovative ideas, better decisions, and greater public support."[2]

In the United States, we tend to let citizen engagement morph into a public veto: *whether* something should be built, rather than *what* should be built. It is a subtle difference, but the framing is important. Our processes largely become forums where people can loudly say "NO!" to something.

Community engagement around land use in the United States tends to be very combative, a legacy of a hundred years of exclusionary zoning and poor planning. (Credit: Mark Ostrow)

No to a duplex in a single-family neighborhood. No to a daycare in a quiet neighborhood. No to affordable housing in our city.

Other than the United States and Canada, most countries don't have single-family zoning. Germany's lowest zoning level allows a mix of uses and small-scale multifamily housing, and it is largely found in villages. Perhaps discussions about growth and housing may be easier because multifamily housing and living in close quarters have been common for generations. As the housing crisis in US cities has gotten more intense and cities allow more types of housing in more of the city, the discussion about planning and participation does seem to shift. I have noticed this in Seattle, where even just a decade ago comments and discussions at planning events were overwhelmingly against any change, but as the city has grown and relegalized more housing in more places, the discussion has drifted and is now about quality of life, access to amenities, increasing affordable housing—all things necessary for a livable city.

District-scale projects such as Hammarby Sjöstad in Stockholm allow cities to better integrate a variety of services and amenities while fostering the creation of high-quality places to live and work. (Credit: Alex Linthicum)

58 Building for People

My experience and research on district planning in Germany is that community participation is oriented less toward saying "no" to projects; instead it leans toward "Yes, and. . . ."

Yes, we understand a new district will be here, *and* we also know that will mean we need a grocery store. *And* we will need mobility connections to reduce car traffic. *And* we would like a café to meet for coffee. *And* we need a primary school to accommodate families. *And* we need quiet and high-quality open space to gather, garden, dine, and so on.

Getting the Public to "Yes, and . . ."

It is important to note who in the public is being engaged. For decades, homeowners in cities—even renter-dominated ones—have had outsized representation at hearings and meetings. Those effects may be related to increasing economic and social segregation. As sociologist Brian McCabe notes, property values correlated to homeowner wealth play a role: "While they are frequently more engaged in their neighborhoods, homeowners often participate in projects that are not necessarily in the best interest of the entire community. Their activism may in fact exacerbate patterns of segregation, increase social exclusion, and create more fractured communities."[3] Cities have even enabled this outsized representation by gatekeeping, through exclusive engagement processes or by having meetings at times difficult for renters, residents who work evenings, or parents to attend. Because of the demographics of ecodistricts (and also transit-oriented development), which skew younger, more diverse, and with more renters, it is important that communities of color, youth, and renters be represented in engagement and planning.

The semantics and processes of land use and planning are obtuse and can be difficult for the public to navigate, especially if they are not familiar with local laws and English is not their first language. Archaic plans that longtime residents may have worked on or know about can be completely inaccessible to younger and newer residents.[4] Community-based organizations can play a role in demystifying the process. Be:Seattle was founded to engage renters through "tenant power workshops" to break down semantic and process barriers, educate them on their rights, and build renter power.[5] To overcome language barriers, some planning departments provide information and engagement in multiple languages. For more inclusive engagement, some planning departments partner with community-based organizations led by people of color.

To meet our housing and climate goals, cities will need to develop districts that are of a high quality. As urban planner Brent Toderian notes, poor planning, something that North American cities have struggled with for decades, increases opposition to housing and urban transformations.[6] Processes that are aligned with diverse, inclusive, and transparent engagement are more likely to lead to positive results. Cities and planning departments that are better able to incorporate the public's innovative ideas and needs into development—getting the public to "yes, and . . ."—will find that their outcomes are more conducive to success.

Co-Creation

In top-down planning, cities or politically connected leaders use their authority to shape development or transformation; perhaps the best example of this is the toxic legacy of federal highways cutting through low-income, largely Black and Brown urban neighborhoods.[7] In bottom-up planning, citizens lead the urban planning of their own districts. There can be disadvantages to this, such as limited access to funds and inability to engage in long-term and comprehensive planning. Pairing top-down and bottom-up processes can allow local needs and knowledge to shine through planning processes that better coordinate long-term and regional plans.

The success of numerous European districts is correlated to urban planning philosophies that balance top-down and bottom-up planning to co-create dense areas with adequate open space, mixed uses, green space, and affordable housing. Vauban's success was tied to both top-down planning from the

Vienna's competitions are run through a top-down/bottom-up model where citizen participation plays an outsized role in the urban planning and the needs of women and children can be prioritized. (Credit: Albert Koch)

60 Building for People

city and bottom-up planning efforts of Forum Vauban, a citizen-led grassroots organization that advocated for the former military barracks to turn into a district prioritizing high-quality urban places, family-friendly housing, low-traffic streets, and ecology.[8] Vienna's Smart City urban planning framework is designed to engage the public at a high degree, also through a top-down/bottom-up approach.[9] This ensures a high level of citizen engagement and incorporation of diverse needs and ideas into concepts and plans. This approach is beneficial as a sort of reality check, and it ensures that politicians and policymakers are collaborating with, not just listening to, the public.

Import IBAs

The Internationale Bauausstellung (IBA, International Building Exhibition) has been an approach using showcase exhibitions for large and complex urban development. Originally conceived in Germany, it has spread in recent years to Switzerland (Basel) and Austria (Vienna). It is more than an exhibition but rather a funded living laboratory for researching and documenting a number of urban conditions, increasingly with a focus on mobility, ecology, and culture.

From 2006 to 2013, the IBA was held in Hamburg, with the organizing assignment being "Developing the city of tomorrow. Where and how do we live, work, study and where will we be in 20 years' time? How will the cities face the impact of climate change?"[10] Public participation in the IBA has evolved into an art form, and formats for the IBA include idea workshops, planning workshops, information sessions, public presentations, roundtables, keynotes, excursions, listening sessions for children and youth, online participation, stakeholder outreach, and public dialogue in planning concepts and competitions.[11] These events allow cities to engage thousands of citizens to work toward the betterment of their existing and proposed neighborhoods.

Hamburg's Oberbillwerder district was part of the IBA and incorporated public participation at multiple levels, from conceptualization to masterplan adoption. After the city's announcement of the goal to build the district, the first event was an informational session with community input on wishes, needs, ideas, and critiques. The second phase was a series of workshops for experts and for a representative citizens' group, as well as engagement opportunities online for those with limited availability. These workshops were to develop topics and themes incorporated into the urban planning competition's brief, culminating the themes of high density, mixed use, and active spaces and neighborhoods. Teams focused on the themes of urban development quality and density; quality of public space; housing and neighborhoods; incorporation of social, education, and cultural places; vibrant and diverse workplaces;

ecology related to climate and energy; mobility concepts and connections; and balance of nature, agriculture; and water management. The third phase was the two-phase competition, incorporating public presentations, discussion events, and workshops in several rounds, where the number of planning teams was reduced based on input from the public dialogue process and expert jury. Oberbillwerder's winning proposal was "the Connected City," by ADEPT with Karres + Brands and Transsolar, who were invited to develop the district's Masterplan and Framework plan, setting rules and regulations on how the district will look.[12] The process of public engagement does not stop there, with public participation processes for the district's Green Loop in addition to building permission phases.

Post-COVID Ramifications

Before COVID, parts of the United States were having a reckoning with their history of public participation being less inclusive and representative.[13]

The masterplan for Hamburg's 290-acre Oberbillwerder district, which will have 7,000 homes and space for 5,000 jobs. The car-light district includes a broad mix of uses, a variety of open spaces, and abundant natural spaces. The Green Loop connects neighborhoods and provides a car-free way to get around while playing a central role in the district's stormwater management. (Credit: By ADEPT and Karres en Brands)

Post-COVID citizen engagement has increasingly moved to digital platforms: social media, surveys, presentations and webinars, online brainstorming, and ideation platforms. These are paths toward increasing engagement from those who opt out of community meetings that have historically been toxic and poorly run, those who do not have the time to attend in-person events, and people for whom travel is difficult.

I don't think it is a coincidence that questions about how development will be oriented in the future—Wie wohnen wir Morgen? (How will we live tomorrow?)—seem to be a nearly constant topic of engagement in European cities. This question requires planning for the future, not upholding the status quo.

Cities change, and ensuring that this change is more equitable and inclusive necessitates meeting people where they are. Ultimately, a public that can have robust and difficult conversations on diversity and inclusion, development, and climate adaptation is necessary. Trust, accountability, and transparency are indispensible for legitimacy and successful engagement.[14] It includes bringing children and young adults into the decision-making process, as in Vienna,[15] because they have needs as well. Perhaps development of federal- or state-funded IBA programs can facilitate innovation and research that the market will not deliver. Planning competitions with citizen dialogues should also be prioritized. Processes and programs that prioritize engagement and co-creation can lead to better, more connected, and more livable ecodistricts.

PART II

Quality of Life and Public Health

CHAPTER 8

Mobility and the District of Short Distances

"By incorporating proximity into cities, the goal is to change the lifestyles of residents—freeing up time, increasing movement through active mobility, enhancing relationships with neighbours, reducing stress— and promote the development of the local economy."[1]

—Professor Carlos Moreno

According to the US Department of Transportation's Bureau of Transportation Statistics, more than half of all trips made in the United States are less than 3 miles.[2] The Federal Highway Administration's data extraction tool shows that trips under 1 mile totaled ten billion miles in 2009.[3] Over half of all car trips are under 3 miles,[4] the sweet spot for cycling. Americans are literally driving climate change, with SUVs and trucks emitting an ever-growing share of those emissions. A 2021 International Energy Agency commentary stated, "If SUVs were an individual country, they would rank *sixth* in the world for absolute emissions in 2021."[5]

Not only are automobiles responsible for a significant percentage of overall carbon emissions, but they are also getting faster, heavier, and deadlier. Tesla has dominated US electric vehicle (EV) sales the last few years, and their 2023 Model 3 Performance Sedan advertises going zero to 60 miles per hour in just 3.1 seconds.[6] The 9,460-pound (4.82-ton!) 2024 GMC Hummer EV pickup can go from zero to 60 in just 3.3 seconds[7] in its WTF mode (apparently that's "Watts to Freedom"). To compare, the 2023 Honda Accord Hybrid weighs only 3,525 pounds, with a zero-to-60 time of 6.5 seconds.[8]

Pedestrian fatalities have returned to levels unseen since the 1980s,[9] eradicating decades of vehicle safety progress. A 2023 Insurance Institute for Highway Safety study found that "vehicles with hoods more than 40 inches off the ground at the leading edge and a grille sloped at an angle of 65 degrees

A climate-forward district prioritizing low-carbon living should be designed so that a five-year-old can safely get around on foot or by bike, as in Munich. (Credit: Heather Eliason)

or less were 45 percent more likely to cause pedestrian fatalities than those with a similar slope and hood heights of 30 inches or less."[10] These are not the cars we grew up playing street hockey around. There has to be a safer, faster, and better way, and it turns out there is: ecodistricts and Carlos Moreno's fifteen-minute city concept.

The Mobilitätswende (mobility transition or turnaround) has been a topic of discussion in German planning for years. The spatial inefficiency of the car has turned out to be a wildly detrimental urban experiment. Ecodistricts and fifteen-minute cities offer the ability to drastically reduce and even eliminate the necessity of car ownership by creating dense, walkable, high-quality environments accessible to daily needs and amenities and connected to broader transportation networks.

Short Distances in the District

Imagine you have two kids. You wake up and get yourself and your kids ready for school. The oldest leaves home, runs into a friend, and they walk five blocks to school together. They don't interact with a single vehicle or street to get there. You walk the youngest to daycare just around the corner from your home. You leave for work, grabbing a quick bite at the local cafe before commuting by tram. At the end of the day, you reverse all of this, stopping at the grocery store that is within walking distance of your home before picking up your youngest from daycare. Even in a city like Seattle, this is largely unheard of. Outside New York City and a handful of urban neighborhoods, the time spent commuting in a car and running errands can add hours to a day.

There are a multitude of co-benefits to sustainable mobility, especially in the ecodistrict. Safer streets for all. Less exposure to air pollution from cars. Less noise pollution—also largely from cars. But the largest co-benefit may be public health. A study published in 2023 noted, "Obesity and physical inactivity have each been associated with increased risk of premature death and cancer in women, but individual-level interventions to increase physical activity and reduce obesity are costly and have short-term effects. Neighborhood walkable spaces are quieter, with better air quality, and can promote walking behaviors, physical activity, and reduce car dependency, which could lead to subsequent improvements in preventing diseases attributed to obesity."[11]

Like transit-oriented development (TOD), the ecodistrict is a dense, walkable neighborhood. The fundamental difference is that the autocentricity of TOD in the United States forces a less enjoyable, less safe, and less healthy environment. The compact nature of the ecodistrict allows it to be a "city of short distances," in a manner that is fundamentally less autocentric. Scaling up to the city, ecodistricts allow a network of linked low-carbon neighborhoods to facilitate low-carbon living at a greater reach. This could be one approach toward achieving Moreno's fifteen-minute city concept, by seeding small districts that could meet the intent and start to mesh into adjacent neighborhoods and each other.

Transit Connectivity

Transit connectivity and having a fast connection to the broader transportation network, whether the district is in the middle of the city or on the outskirts, is key to the viability of the ecodistrict. Freiburg, Germany's former chief planner, Wulf Daseking, was instrumental in spearheading a framework of policies that have guided several new districts where car-free and car-light living are not only possible but thriving. Freiburg's spatial planning policies require the incorporation of transit to connect these districts with the city. Daseking was co-author of "The Freiburg Charter," a framework for developing urban planning policies based on twelve principles. Spatial principle number IV is *urban development along public transportation lines*, and it states,

> Public transport must be closely tied to any urban development concept and must be given general priority over personal means of transport. The objective is to carefully and consistently increase urban density along public transport routes and to locate services around the stops of tram lines or other public transport nodes which have a central function and high user frequency.

Freiburg is an interesting leader in the development of car-light ecodistricts. The planning of its nearly car-free district of Vauban began in the 1990s. The lesser-known district of Rieselfeld offers a more socially mixed and urban template for car-light urbanism, with 25 percent of the homes being social housing. The Dietenbach district, also aiming to be car-light with a high quality of life, is in planning. With a minimum of 50 percent of homes intended to be social housing,[12] along with prioritization of other forms of nonmarket housing such as coops and Baugruppen, it will have an even broader demographic mix than previous districts. Vauban, Rieselfeld, and (soon) Dietenbach are all tram-oriented districts, with strong bike connections to surrounding neighborhoods and downtown.

Larger cities tend to have regional or high-speed rail connecting the district. The location of these stations varies: It can be at the edge of the district, as at

Hamburg's Oberbillwerder or Vienna's Seestadt Aspern, or it can cut through the middle, as in Stockholm's Hammarby Sjöstad.

Walkability First

Some of the biggest barriers to reducing car trips in the United States are school and daycare runs, with the *Washington Post* identifying 53 percent of students being driven to school in 2022.[13] Vienna's Seestadt was planned with preschools and daycares in the district to accommodate new families. The intent is an easy choice for a sustainable mode of travel to drop off and pick up children before continuing on to work or home. These routes are designed so that children generally don't cross major streets, and there are safe and quiet routes for them to walk, bike, or roll around their neighborhood. Naturally, the primary school features abundant bicycle parking, but we were amazed to see the number of scooters parked outside on a mild spring day.

When Vienna undertakes planning of new districts, gender mainstreaming, a strategy towards societal gender equity, is prioritized.[14] The city acknowledges that women and mothers tend to do an outsized proportion of invisible

The scale of streets in the district should be right-sized for foot traffic, bicycles, and other forms of slow, sustainable mobility, as on this street in Amsterdam. (Credit: Mark Ostrow)

70 Building for People

In Stockholm's Hammarby Sjöstad, streets for cars and logistics prioritize safety and accessibility over speed. (Credit: Alex Linthicum)

labor. One way to reduce this burden is to make travel distances as safe and short as possible, creating a "city of short distances."

A meta-analysis of policies and interventions successfully reducing car usage in EU cities can be found in ecodistricts.[15] These interventions include limiting vehicular traffic access, designating car-free streets, providing bicycle and pedestrian infrastructure, integrating carsharing into districts, and working with schools to develop and promote car-free transit to school.

The Wohnstrasse

As cities have diverse street types (boulevards, collectors, arterials, neighborhood streets), so do most ecodistricts. Along with pedestrian and bike routes for low-carbon mobility, there are often a multitude of (traffic-calmed) streets. In Freiburg's Vauban, the streets branching off the 19 miles per hour (30 kilometers per hour) main collector street are *Spielstrassen* (play streets) that see little car usage, with a low-traffic, low-stress shared street where pedestrians and cyclists have priority and cars are generally limited to 7 miles per hour (10 kilometers per hour). This is somewhat similar to a *Woonerf* (living street), a traffic-calmed residential-only shared street (the variation of a traffic-calmed shared street with businesses is a *Winkelerf*).

E-Bikes Are Game Changers

For the longest time, I wrote off electric bicycles, thinking the electric assist was not needed. However, with two growing kids playing sports around the region, it was no longer an option to just rely on my "acoustic" cargo bike. I wish I had converted earlier. For longer distances, it saves an incredible amount of time. The electric assist flattens hills—a massive benefit in a city with varied topography, such as Seattle—and I barely sweat while riding. On top of being significantly less expensive than an EV, the e-bike is an underappreciated game changer when it comes to sustainable mobility. This was very noticeable when we lived in Bayern, where most users were elderly riders getting around town with ease. E-bikes have incredibly small carbon footprints, are relatively lightweight, and are typically faster door to door than driving for short distances. Today, the advantages of electric bikes are quite apparent, even without cities leading on Vision Zero and safe streets, and they have routinely outsold electric cars in the United States by significant margins for several years.[16]

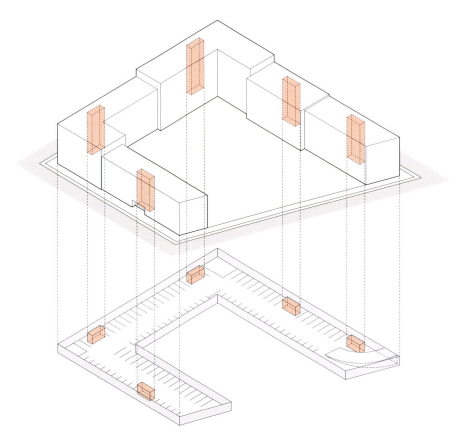

In the United States, massive parking garages above grade, in the courtyard, or below grade are generally constructed on a building-by-building basis, increasing the number of access ramps and overall costs. European districts still have parking; however, it is often located in shared or collated underground parking garages that access all or several buildings on the block. (Credit: Michael Eliason/Larch Lab)

72 Building for People

District Logistics

Delivery vans are the lifeblood of urban areas the world over, and with the introduction of zero-emission zones, low-traffic neighborhoods, and electric vans, their environmental footprint is at least somewhat reduced. However, cargo bikes and e-cargo bikes are the secret ingredient to decarbonized last-mile solutions in urban areas. A 2015 CycleLogistics study found that in European cities, "on average 51% of all motorised trips—associated with the transport of goods—could be shifted from car to the bicycle or cargo bicycle."[17] A study led by the University of Westminster's Active Transit Academy after the adoption of London's Ultra Low Emission Zone noted that cargo bike deliveries were faster than vans but less expensive to operate and maintain and resulted in better environments for both drivers and pedestrians.[18] I'm not sure why US policy on cycle logistics is at least a decade behind EU policy, but there is ample potential for improvement in urban areas.

The SeestadtFLOTTE is Seestadt Aspern's affordable bike share fleet that includes e-bikes and e-cargo bikes.[19] The fleet started small and has increased over the years as more housing has been completed. In addition, two cargo bikes can be borrowed for free from the district's management office. These programs allow people to move kids and goods easily around the district and wider neighborhood. It's also an opportunity for residents and businesses to test different e-bicycle options. Most people in dense urban areas don't have the need or space to store cargo bikes, so having the ability to easily rent or borrow one on the rare occasion it is needed can go a long way to reducing overall car trips.

Tram logistics might be something beyond one's wildest transit fantasies, but is a topic I was introduced to while traveling in Dresden, where the CarGo Tram operated on the city's tram lines. It carried freight to Volkswagen's Transparency Factory, although service ended in 2020 due to economic inefficiencies.[20] Frankfurt, and most recently Vienna, have completed pilot projects using tram logistics with cargo bike–sized pallets for sustainable last-mile delivery.[21]

Child-Friendly Routes

Mobility for children and older adults within the district can be planned so that there are few interactions with cars and other vehicles. Pedestrian zones in commercial areas, with limited hours for deliveries, are common. Hamburg's Oberbillwerder district will feature a Green Loop, a car-free path circumnavigating the district connecting play areas, schools, daycare facilities, recreation areas, and the district's five neighborhoods. The loop features space

Cargo bikes, and other forms of micromobility, are the future of low-carbon logistics in urban areas. (Credit: Michael Eliason)

for nature and is also part of the stormwater mitigation of the district.[22] This would entail parents walking or biking to school or daycare and then on to the local transit stop without having to interact with cars at all. In Vienna's Sonnwendviertel, the school campus is located in the middle of the district and can be reached from most buildings without crossing any streets. A few sections may have to cross one or two single-lane low-traffic streets. Daycare facilities are also reached in a similar manner, with several private and city-run options in the district—an option we would have preferred over driving to daycare with our young kids.

Carsharing

Carsharing is a form of shared mobility that operates through the short-term rental or usage of a vehicle. It can be a great tool for reducing the reliance on cars, allowing residents to use a vehicle when transit, cycling, or walking isn't possible. Zipcar, a round-trip carshare company, is one of the better-known options in the United States, featuring dedicated parking spaces and the ability to rent various types of cars for a set time or day. In Seattle, we've used AAA's GIG floating carshare program sporadically since the pandemic in order to avoid buying a car.

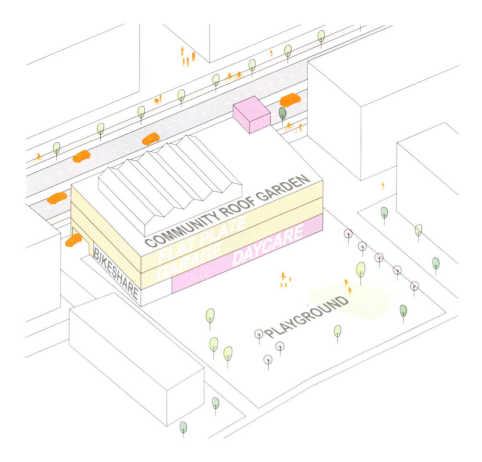

Mobility hubs can serve as flexible parking garages, with uses that can evolve over time as car ownership and usage decrease. This can include bikeshare and bike repair shops, daycare facilities, community amenities, youth centers, and other symbiotic functions. (Credit: Michael Eliason/Larch Lab)

In Bayern, we had a cooperative carshare program that was an affordable round-trip option paid by cost-based user fees. Similar cooperative programs have been used in a number of ecodistricts in Europe. Vienna's Seestadt includes three different options: a self-organized nonprofit option, another run by the Austrian railroad company, and WienMobil Auto, run by Vienna's transportation line (annual card holders get a 10 percent discount). The latter seems quite a deal, with rental rates[23] of €2.60 per hour. In Seattle both Zipcar and GIG carshare cost significantly more.

Developers have been incorporating carshare into their buildings for years, as a means of weaning residents off cars, and it's been so successful that even suburban townhome development[24] is incorporating carshare schemes. We've discussed buying an electric minivan when our Baugruppe gets built, which would be available for shared use so residents can live car-free.

Mobility Hubs

The mobility hub is a focal point of a transportation network for the district, where multiple modes of mobility come together. It can be where regional or local transit enters the district. There is typically space for bicycle parking, e-bike sharing, carsharing, and other forms of e-mobility. Charging points for e-bikes and EVs are increasingly common, as are bicycle repair shops, parcel lockers, and drop boxes. Some include additional functions such as youth centers, corner stores, or cafés. Larger districts, such as Berlin's Schumacher Quartier—a massive ecodistrict near Berlin's now-defunct Tegel airport that will have homes for up to 10,000 people and space for 20,000 jobs—may have several mobility hubs interspersed throughout.

Infrastructure can serve multiple uses. In Vienna's Seestadt, the area under the elevated U-bahn network provides play areas protected from the rain, as well as adjacent bike and rolling paths. (Credit: Lukasz Karnas)

Munich's Freiham district, on the city's outskirts, is planning to incorporate tandem uses in the common above-grade garages distributed around the district. These uses include daycare facilities. The roofs could be community amenities, programmed for gardens, sports facilities, playgrounds, or other recreation. The mobility concepts at Freiham will form a template that Munich deploys in future districts.[25]

Futureproofing Mobility

It is important that districts have the capacity to adapt to new forms of mobility in the future. The mobility sector has changed dramatically in the last decade, and as governments move to curb their transportation emissions

76 Building for People

more rapidly to meet climate goals, there will probably be a number of innovative and potentially disruptive solutions, hopefully ones that enable and facilitate more walking, rolling, and bicycling. Electric scooter shares have overtaken electric bike shares in many US cities,[26] and although we prefer biking, many friends and colleagues find e-scooters quite enjoyable to use. Drone logistics, with numerous and valid concerns about safety, visual pollution, and privacy, is being pioneered in several locations and may offer significant emission savings for deliveries.[27] Autonomous microtransit may loop through the district, connecting residents with their homes, businesses, communal amenities, mobility hubs, and the wider transit networks.

Providing wide bicycle streets or shared paths with direct routes allows a certain level of flexibility for the unknown. Mobility hubs and parking garages can be planned to be circular and demountable, so that if the garage is no longer necessary, it can be completely dismantled, with components being reused elsewhere. Gensler Research Institute notes that in order to maximize flexibility for future reuse, parking garages should be designed with flat parking levels and higher ceilings.[28]

Although car reduction should be the goal, innovations in car parking such as this stacking system can reduce the overall carbon footprint. (Credit: WÖHR Autoparksysteme GmbH)

Parking

Wondering why I have saved the issue of car parking for last? Frankly, the private automobile should have the lowest priority in the ecodistrict. The issues of car use and parking are not really different in European cities; car ownership rates just tend to be much lower. However, with well-planned districts, it may be possible to achieve car ownership rates outside the downtown core or even in suburban settings that match EU urban ownership rates. Most

Mobility and the District of Short Distances 77

European ecodistricts still, much to my dismay, build a significant amount of parking. Street parking is fairly common, although typically far less, leaving more space for trees or other forms of mobility.

In TOD, parking is handled primarily on a building-by-building basis. The approach varies widely, but buildings with underground parking extending several levels below grade are incredibly common. Also common is the "Texas doughnut," a single-loaded apartment wrapping around an above-grade parking garage where most countries would place a courtyard. From a cost standpoint, building several levels of underground parking results in high embodied carbon emissions, and they are not futureproofed for drops in car ownership. The Texas doughnut is also an urban planning abomination: Residents lose the opportunity for a courtyard, the benefits of ventilation and daylight in single-loaded corridor layouts, and the ability to convert the garage to other uses.

In most European ecodistricts, collated garages are becoming the norm. At the block level, these are typically one- or two-level underground garages with either a separate pedestrian access point or vertical connections to each building's entry. Many districts also use above-grade common garages that can be used for several blocks or a small neighborhood. These can be positioned along the perimeter or distributed within the district. I prefer this approach over underground parking for a number of reasons. First, it costs less than building a collated underground garage, because the structure is more uniform. Second, the construction results in less embodied carbon emissions, and further reductions can be achieved through prefabrication. Third, they are easy to replace or retrofit for other uses when private car ownership drops and car parking is no longer needed. In 2020, a team led by Copenhagen-based JaJa architects won a competition for a mass timber mobility hub in Aarhus, Denmark.[29] The mobility hub features three levels of car parking over two levels of shops, cafés, and workshops and is planned so that as car usage decreases, retail and community spaces can take over the former parking levels.

Parking management also plays a role. Pricing must be such that visitors can find spots. Parking should be decoupled from rents to ensure fairness for residents who do not own or need a car.

Sustainable mobility will become increasingly important as cities strive to meet Vision Zero, safe street goals, and sustainability metrics. The success of the fifteen-minute city and ecodistricts will hinge on cities prioritizing active and sustainable modes of transit to foster safe, vibrant, walkable environments.

CHAPTER 9

A Good Economic and Social Mix

There is no standard definition of social housing, and according to the Organisation for Economic Co-operation and Development, it may be developed and managed across a broad spectrum including public developers and non-profit, limited profit, private, and cooperative entities.[1] I tend to use it as a phrase that covers all forms of nonmarket housing, including cooperatives, cohousing, and Baugruppen.

Vienna's extensive history of social housing is rooted in the rise of its social democratic party after World War I, and today it has one of the most robust social housing programs in the world. Nearly 60 percent of residents live in affordable or social housing,[2] and the way affordable housing is tied into Vienna's urban planning and development is exemplary.

Ensuring new districts have a good economic and social mix of residents and mix of functions was foundational to Vienna's Smart City urban planning strategy. The city's Bauträgerwettbewerbe (developer competitions) are a critical component of achieving high-quality, dense, and livable housing and neighborhoods. Teams compete to develop and receive land and subsidies for individual projects and are judged by a diverse panel on the economics of the project, the architecture, the ecology of the building, and the social mix.[3] The city has effectively leveraged its purse to keep the price of construction low while making developers compete on the merits and economics. This results in buildings that are incredibly innovative and urban development that takes the needs of people into account rather than letting the economics of market rate development dictate how development is shaped.

In Paris, the 133-acre mixed-use Clichy-Batignolles ecodistrict consists of 3,400 homes, with half reserved as social housing and another 20 percent as rent-restricted apartments. These homes are arranged on car-light streets around the 25-acre Martin Luther King Parc in the middle of the district, which doubles as stormwater and urban heat island mitigation.[4]

Berlin's ambitious mass timber Schumacher Quartier, near Tegel, is planning up to 50 percent of the 5,000 planned homes for social and student housing, with cooperatives and Baugruppen making up another 40 percent.[5] This means that the mixed-use district will be composed primarily of working- and middle-class households. Like Clichy-Batignolles, this 118-acre car-light district features a massive park surrounded by mixed-use and mixed-tenure blocks with a combination of semipublic and private courtyards.

Munich uses a program called the München-Modell (Munich Model), requiring a certain mix of homes, which was used in Ackermannbogen, a mixed-use district where nonmarket housing makes up nearly half of the dwellings. Twenty percent are affordable rentals, nearly 30 percent are middle-class rentals and condos, and the balance are market-rate homes. This district also includes a wide variety of homes, from rowhouses to small towers, several

Vienna's Sonnwendviertel is composed of midrise and highrise buildings with a broad spectrum of tenures. Although there is market-rate housing, the majority of homes are nonmarket housing, including social housing, subsidized housing, Baugruppen, student housing, and cluster apartments. This allows for a broader social mix of residents compared with transit-oriented development, where most housing is market-rate apartments. (Credit: Mark Ostrow)

Transit-oriented development is often limited to a narrow area around bus-rapid transit or major transit stops. (Credit: Steven Vance)

cooperatives, and Baugruppen. Children under fifteen years old make up a quarter of the residents, and the district includes a school, daycare facilities, abundant green space, and low-traffic streets.[6]

The City of Vienna has been building ecological districts of various sizes for roughly twenty years, and social housing has been a significant component of them. In 2018, Vienna's government passed legislation that all new residential or mixed-use districts, or rezones with residential area greater than 5,000 square meters (roughly fifty homes), would require two thirds to be affordable.[7] Vienna's government realizes that the benefits of compact, urban development are even more beneficial to those with limited income and has spent much of the last century developing processes to prioritize mixed-use districts with a rather robust economic and social mix of residents.

Ensuring a greater mix of affordable and social housing in the district can counteract gentrification and exclusion. This social mix does not have to happen at the building level, which is what US cities attempt to achieve with block-scaled transit-oriented development. Cities in other countries

aim to achieve a good economic and social mix at the neighborhood and the block level, not solely at the building level. This is a significant benefit of the small-scale urban development made possible with midrise point access blocks and where urban blocks are made up of six to fifteen different buildings instead of one or two. This approach also allows for much more diversity and flexibility in achieving the mix. Another approach would be to require a better balance between owned and rented homes. The majority of dwellings in transit-oriented development are rentals, and opportunities for owned middle-class housing are rare.

Increasing Inclusive Housing

Inclusion needs to be part of the discussion of the social mix, as does accessibility. According to the Centers for Disease Control and Prevention, more than one quarter of US residents have a disability.[8] An analysis of housing in the United States found that less than a quarter of a percent of all homes were fully accessible for wheelchair users, and only 4 percent of all homes were accessible.[9] Disabled renters are also in a more tenuous situation, because

Seattle's Passive House Social Housing Public Development Authority is tasked with building mixed-income social housing, similar to the approach taken in Vienna. (Credit: Lukasz Karnas)

housing shortages nationally drive median rent.[10] US federal and state policies give a baseline for accessible housing; however, these are incredibly insufficient and are only as good as the enforcement. Because of the peculiarities of how we build, most new multifamily housing in the United States is not adaptable either.

The high cost of elevators compared with that in European countries also plays a role, because it precludes more accessible or adaptable housing from being built in low-rise buildings and missing middle housing. Prioritizing and legalizing taller point access blocks is one approach to constructing more dwellings that can be adaptable. Concept tendering can also be used to increase inclusive housing and foster more inclusive districts. This method has been used successfully in several inclusive projects in Hamburg, Freiburg, and Vienna. Lastly, incentivizing, or better yet adopting, standards for more inclusive design, such as The Kelsey's Inclusive Design Standards,[11] can also set the bar higher than the minimum requirements set by the federal government.

In Seattle, which has a deep and growing homeless crisis,[12] a citizen-led effort for a Social Housing Public Development Authority (PDA) was passed in 2023 (Initiative 135).[13] The PDA is tasked with building social housing that meets the Passive House standard or buying existing buildings to rehabilitate and remove from the housing market. I worked closely with the organizers of the initiative to get the Passive House focus added, because I knew the climate and public health benefits were so much greater than any other building standard out there.

A few months after the social housing initiative passed, I ended up as a founding board member for the PDA,[14] and we are slowly moving forward to build a more equitable city.

CHAPTER 10

Urban Places and Spaces

The public realm is the district's living room, serving a multitude of functions: a place for planned and impromptu social gatherings and circulation through the district. It shapes how civic life unfolds and where people eat, debate, shop, socialize, and play. Public spaces should be social meeting places as well as spaces for movement. The public realm of a district should include diverse places and spaces. These should be spaces that are inclusive and accessible for all.

Well-designed public space not only is necessary for placemaking but is critical for accessibility and facilitating sustainable mobility. Accessible routes and places are needed to ensure inclusive and safer ways to get around. Streets that are too loud or dangerous will see little activation. Squares and plazas that are not designed with climate and comfort in mind are not pleasant places to linger. Routes for walking and rolling that are circuitous, while streets for cars are direct, send conflicting signals about priorities. There should be a hierarchy of streets, with abundant and fast connections for walking or rolling. Connections through the district where cars are prioritized should be minimized to reduce traffic.

Relying on private actors to provide a public amenity is rife for abuse and exclusion. Privately owned public spaces (POPS) are a form of tradeoff—private developers will include "publicly accessible" open space for some sort of height or floor area ratio bonus or a tax break—but the accessibility of these types of spaces is heavily contested or even ignored. As Christian Dimmer notes, there are also discontinuities in the application of POPS, as when Japanese developers add a sidewalk in front of a building for increased building area, but the sidewalk does not connect to a wider network.[1] The pandemic has also exposed a number of weaknesses of POPS, especially when they are located above grade or when it's necessary to enter a building to access them.[2]

Access to frequent transit, a low-stress network, and barrier-free design make for a high-quality public realm in Vienna's Nordbahnhof district. (Credit: Lukasz Karnas)

The public realm should be designed to promote sustainability and active modes of travel. Paths connecting different neighborhoods or quarters of the

district should prioritize walking, biking, and rolling. Increasingly, districts are incorporating pedestrian paths to circumnavigate the district without interacting with vehicles at all. A larger Quartiersplatz—a district plaza—is common and typically associated with a more commercial or mixed nature of the district. Larger ecodistricts have smaller plazas incorporated into neighborhoods, offering meeting points or even places for smaller commercial enterprises. Pedestrian zones in the more commercial and mixed parts of a district are also opportunities for high-quality public realms. Designed by landscape architecture firm YEWO, Vienna's Sonnwendviertel incorporates

Top, A pedestrian network connecting residents with schools, pedestrian streets, parks, and open space away from busier car-centric streets creates a much quieter and delightful method to get around. (Credit: Albert Koch)

Lower, In Seestadt, modal filters allow residents to conveniently access ground floor retail and restaurants without driving. (Credit: Lukasz Karnas)

a pedestrianized Bloch-Bauer-Promenade running parallel to the 37-acre Helmut-Zilk-Park on the urban eastern half of the district, with pedestrianized streets perpendicular to the promenade connecting and expanding the public realm into the park.[3] The promenade allows for a safe, urban, and high-quality public connection running the length of the district, connecting residents, commercial enterprises, offices, nonprofits, and community amenities.

Ground Floor Activation

Fostering lively and active ground floor zones is a bit of an art. How people interact with these zones, the buildings, and each other can amplify the quality and attractiveness of the public realm. Often in transit-oriented development, the focus is mostly on ground floor retail, with little variation between commercial and residential areas, because most buildings are mixed-use residential with ground floor commercial spaces. Residential or predominantly residential areas are common even in large ecodistricts. These places still maintain a high level of walkability and include a public realm and mix of uses but often at a more intimate scale. This can even include spaces for businesses or offices in addition to cafés, restaurants, or bakeries for daily needs.

Another aspect of transit-oriented development that could greatly be improved is providing ground floor space for nonmarket needs: affordable co-working

Larger city blocks allow for creative ways to access individual buildings and turn the community's focus to its green center, as in this proposal in Växjö. (Credit: Kjellander Sjöberg with +imgs, www.plusimgs.com)

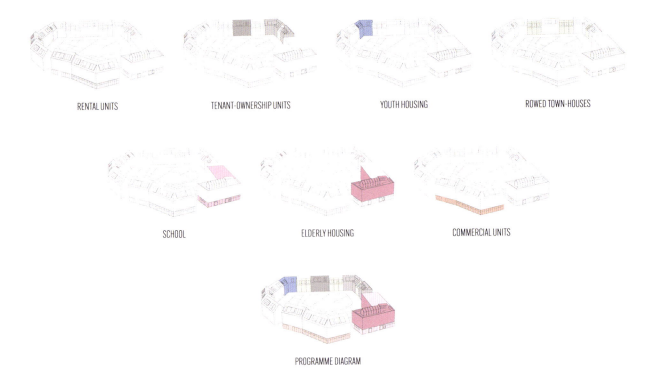

places, community and meeting rooms, offices and spaces for small medical uses, and spaces for city agencies and social organizations. Like many projects, Stuttgart's 6-acre Am Rotweg district has a special focus on ground floor activation for social benefit and community. ISSS research | architecture | urbanism's plan includes numerous market and nonmarket uses for this district, intended for a broad and inclusive feel. These uses include a daycare, youth center, workshop spaces, sports fields, a dance theater, a district kitchen, co-working spaces, offices, cafés, a mobility hub with a bike workshop, guest apartments, a playground, and a large district square in the middle of the block.[4]

Rethinking Access

Using larger city blocks can allow for creativity and rethinking of the typical approach to development. In Växjö, Sweden, Kjellander Sjöberg Architects won the planning competition for the Skärvet neighborhood block. It features a ring of buildings of varying heights around an existing green space with several trees. The block is composed of several different housing types: townhomes, apartments, condominiums, housing for youth, and an elderly care facility.[5] The buildings are entered from the courtyard side of the block, inverting the typical approach, positioning the park and lively common area at the literal and visual center of the community, and potentially inducing more social interaction. Ground floor commercial anchors the block's corner with a café, spilling into the interior of the courtyard.

Fine-grained urbanism allows for diverse functions and housing types while allowing access to green space and fostering community interactions. (Credit: Kjellander Sjöberg)

Open space and the public realm must also provide shade and respite from the elements while allowing people to gather outdoors. Seating areas with pergolas, trees, or other shading devices should be incorporated or deployable for periods of intense heat. A low percentage of the district should be sealed surfaces, further reducing heat islands and aiding in stormwater management. Splash parks and spray parks can be places to cool down and avoid overheating. Paving and hardscape materials can be selected to reduce urban heat islands and embodied carbon. As with buildings, the embodied carbon of landscapes and hardscapes is ripe for decarbonization. In 2019, under the direction of Vienna's deputy mayor Birgit Hebein, Vienna started piloting a network of "cool streets" with misters, shaded areas, lighter paving surfaces, and seating for community events.[6]

Adequate shade from trees and buildings will become more important in providing comfortable paths through the city in a warming world. (Credit: Lukasz Karnas)

In keeping with the theme of flexibility, it is not possible to program every square inch of a district's public space. Space should be provided that is unprogrammed and could host a variety of uses, including pop-ups, food trucks, festivals, or community events. There may even be the possibility of prototyping small startup spaces where small businesses can be incubated.

Urban Places and Spaces 89

CHAPTER 11

Opportunities for New Forms of Living

Household formation today is incredibly diverse and varied. The "nuclear family" is at the lowest level of popularity in fifty years,[1] with just 37 percent of all adults twenty-five to forty-nine years old living with their spouse and at least one child. Forty-five percent of adults eighteen to twenty-nine years old are living at home with their parents.[2] The very definition of *family* is shifting, and with single-family houses increasingly unattainable, there should be a broad mix of affordable housing choices to accommodate these shifting demographics.

The US housing stock increasingly consists of either small apartments in massive buildings or detached houses, with little in between—an issue exacerbated by poor planning and financing regimes. A lack of housing diversity can lead to increased foreclosures in economic downturns[3] and is making it harder for the Silver Tsunami—the wave of aging Baby Boomers—to find adequate housing in retirement.[4] Our housing homogeneity leads to many issues, including a lack of affordable housing options, autocentric neighborhoods, racial segregation, and a lack of community connectedness that amplifies the social isolation and loneliness crisis.

Many European cities are all in on fostering diverse housing types and new forms of living. Their building and zoning codes are nowhere near as restrictive as US codes are, allowing for much more heterogeneity in housing types (see Chapter 5). Local governments also play a more active role in land politics, often controlling more land than most US cities. At the scale of a single building there tends to be a much broader mix of dwelling sizes (not just studios but three- and even four-bedroom homes) and unit types; flats, maisonettes (apartments spanning two or more floors), and ground-oriented townhomes all coexist. Cities have oriented land use regulations and urban policies to allow and incentivize new forms of collective dwelling, including Baugruppen, cooperatives, Clusterwohnungen (cluster apartments), multigenerational housing, and more. This diversity can foster a broad economic and social mix of residents and result in more livable districts and buildings.

In Seattle's Capitol Hill neighborhood, a courtyard with access to the common house is the heart of Capitol Hill Urban Cohousing. Units on either side are dual aspect, with daylight on opposite sides, and are able to cross-ventilate, strengthening environmental and social resiliency. (Credit: Schemata Workshop, Inc.)

In the United States, cooperatives are rare outside a handful of places such as New York, and cohousing is an even smaller niche, although there are some notable urban examples. One of these is Schemata Workshop's Capitol Hill Urban Cohousing, a small mixed-use multigenerational midrise in Seattle's Capitol Hill. The dwellings are situated at the front and rear of the parcel, with a courtyard in the middle, adjacent unit access, and stairway, allowing all units to cross-ventilate. The common house, where community meals and events are taken, is located directly off this central courtyard. Capitol Hill Urban Cohousing is an exemplary model of how point access blocks work well, even for infill lots.[5] With better regulations, we could have entire blocks filled with incredible buildings like this.

Eastern Village Cohousing in Silver Spring, Maryland, is another urban cohousing project, with fifty-five homes of a variety of sizes. It also has numerous amenity spaces including a common house for community events and meals, kids' playroom, exercise room, workshop, game room, roof deck, and guest rooms. Notably, it was also an office-to-residential conversion, long before they became popular.[6]

Baugruppen are virtually nonexistent, although I have spent the better part of a decade trying to build a movement around them as what middle-class housing could look like. There are a handful of Baugruppe-adjacent projects in New York City, initiated mostly by Loading Dock 5 architects.[7] There are growing movements for social housing and community land trusts, but these remain rare.

Rezoning areas of detached homes for small multifamily housing has been one of the main approaches cities and states have used to address their housing crises, though as noted in Chapter 6, states are looking at rethinking other regulations to unlock more housing. This has been followed by a surge of interest in small-scale multifamily housing that was common before the widespread adoption of single-family zoning in the 1920s: duplexes, triplexes, rowhouses, courtyard apartments, and more. The urban planning firm Opticos has labeled these housing types that are generally three stories or less and compatible with detached houses the missing middle. It's important to note that one of the reasons these types have been rare since the adoption of comprehensive zoning in the 1920s and 1930s is that they were made illegal through increasingly prohibitive zoning restrictions.

Although the focus to reintroduce these missing types is needed and long overdue, zoning alone is not the reason these are rare today. Many larger cities have delayed action for so long that between land costs and housing

In Seattle, missing middle housing may provide compatibility with detached houses, but poor regulation can induce autocentric neighborhoods with reduced tree canopy, limited space for biodiversity, and no means to mitigate urban heat islands. (Credit: Luke Gardner)

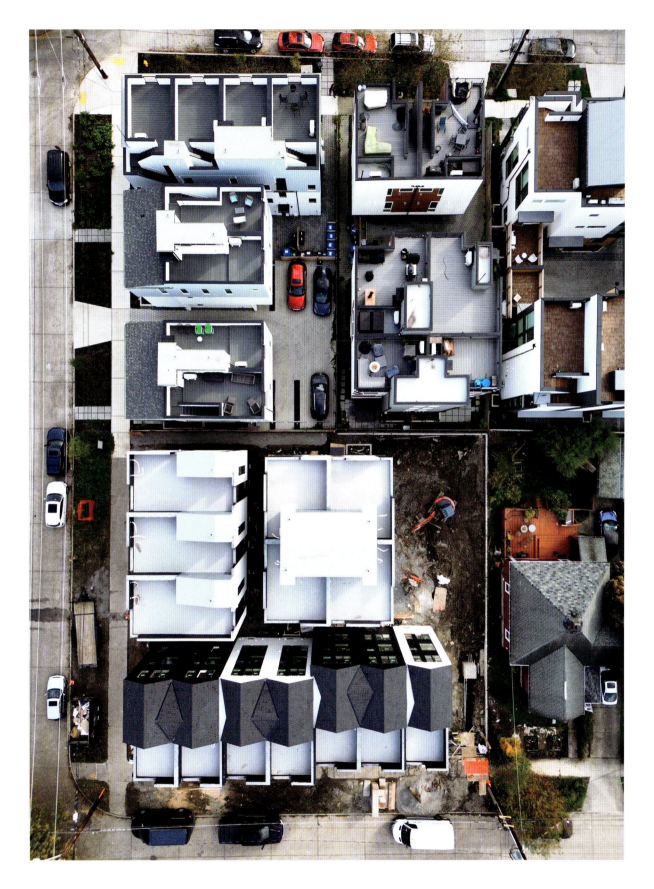

Opportunities for New Forms of Living 93

construction, missing middle projects usually are not economically feasible. Existing residents opposed to new housing have also played in role in exacerbating systemic housing shortages. Additionally, in many cities, the housing shortage is so great that even a significant increase in small-scale developments such as accessory dwelling units and small apartment buildings will have little effect. Housing shortages in other countries have led to creativity and innovation in fostering new types of living. Financing opportunities for innovative projects also exist, including through ethical banks such as Germany's cooperative bank GSL, which had funded the majority of projects for the Mietshaeuser Syndikat (rental house syndicate). These new forms of living have largely skipped the United States, perhaps in part because the United States is late to the housing crisis, or perhaps because of cultural effects.

Fostering a broad range of new forms of urban living could provide new paths for affordable and livable dwellings. Inducing more varied, sufficient, community-oriented, and affordable housing opportunities than our status quo allows, especially at the district scale, opens up a multitude of opportunities. These forms of self-organized dwelling are also becoming quite common in European ecodistricts, including some neighborhoods where they are prioritized over market-rate development.

Freiburg's car-light Vauban ecodistrict is filled with numerous Baugruppen, providing middle-class housing in quiet, lush neighborhoods. (Credit: Payton Chung)

Baugruppen

Baugruppen (German: building groups) are self-developed urban cohousing, where future residents come together and pool their resources to collectively plan and develop their own homes. These can be developed on land they purchase, previously owned, or rented long term through a ground lease. They are an appealing and more affordable alternative for those wishing to live in cities, near friends, family, and jobs. They also offer the chance for residents to select the amenities they want and the level of sustainability and climate adaptability they would like to prioritize when government mandates and the market cannot. Baugruppen can offer accessible, family-friendly homes for a mix of household types and generations, contributing to a high quality of life and well-being. These projects tend to be of a much higher build quality at a lower cost than market-rate development, thanks to the elimination of developer profit and marketing costs. The Dutch have a form of development similar to Baugruppen, called the Collectief Particulier Opdrachtgeverschap (collective private commissioning). In many US cities, these forms of development could result in significant savings (from 10 to 20 percent) over market-rate housing.

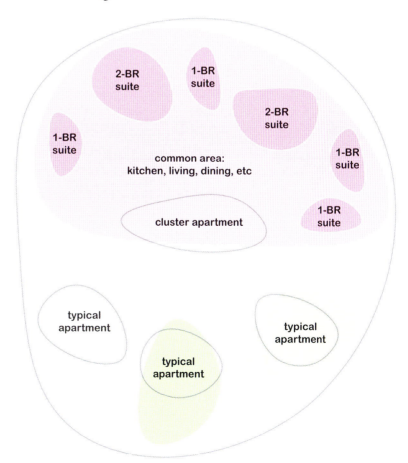

Cluster apartments allow for communal living with a focus on adequate common space, paired with private space. Many suites incorporate a small gallery with a tea kitchen for more private engagement with guests or for getting ready in the morning. (Credit: Michael Eliason/Larch Lab)

Opportunities for New Forms of Living 95

I first saw Baugruppen while working in Freiburg, where more than half of Vauban's plots were reserved for them by the city and sold at cost to interested groups. Several innovative projects were completed here, including one of the first multifamily Passive House buildings, in addition to one of the first mass timber multifamily buildings. After our first child was born, I realized we were priced out of Seattle's housing market if we wanted to live the kind of car-free or car-light lifestyle we had in Europe. We had no desire to live in a three- or four-story townhouse, and we started to research the feasibility of developing a family-friendly, car-light Baugruppe in Seattle. Although this project is on hold because of land costs and high interest rates, our group thinks we have figured out an approach for developing a Passive House point access block Baugruppe with a variety of unit types in the next year or two.

Cluster Apartments

The concept of the Clusterwohnung (cluster apartment) is a hybrid between a small apartment and a shared residence. It is collective living intended to maximize common space while remaining affordable. The cluster apartment is becoming common in districts throughout Germany and Switzerland, and the federal governments of both countries have studied[8] and promoted these diverse arrangements for several years. It is a supersized apartment with several small, self-contained bedroom suites. The suites usually consist of a small anteroom, a tea kitchen, and a private bathroom. The typical common spaces—kitchen, living, dining—are generally much larger than in average apartments, to accommodate the greater number of residents. The suites can all be for singles, but some of the more inclusive projects in Swiss cooperatives include larger suites that can accommodate new parents, single parents, and elderly residents. These offer opportunities for multigenerational living and housing for people with disabilities. Meals are often shared but are not required to be.

Mehr als Wohnen (German: More than Living) is a district full of cooperatives, built on the Hunziker Areal redevelopment in the north of Zurich. The development features a number of incredible projects, but perhaps the most interesting is Duplex Architekten's House A, a building full of Clusterwohnungen. Common areas of each dwelling include generous kitchen and dining areas, smaller seating and living areas dispersed between the suites, and sizable outdoor balconies. There are laundry and drying rooms on each level, space for a guest restroom, and bicycle and unit storage. According to a report on the district, initial rents for the largest cluster apartments, 400 square meters (4,300 square feet) with 13.5 rooms (six suites with seven bedrooms total), were listed at 7,730 CHF.[9] The net rent on these apartments works out to 19.30 CHF per square meter, or roughly half the rent of a one-bedroom apartment in new construction in Zurich.[10]

As the housing crisis has unfolded, there has been an interesting glimpse into how market conditions can influence collective living. Various co-living schemes have been promoted or built, though few offer the quality of collective living found in cluster apartments, with significantly smaller common areas and little affordability. Co-buying schemes also exist. One of the more interesting examples is that of four single mothers who purchased a fourplex in Washington, DC, at the height of the pandemic.[11] They were unable to individually purchase their own homes, but they put their money together and were able to buy a fourplex where they could support each other. Cities need more opportunities for community building and affordable housing like this.

In Seattle, a handful of developers built quasicluster apartments, consisting of small sleeping suites with a kitchenette and bathroom. However, unlike in the cluster apartments found throughout much of Europe, the common spaces for these projects were incredibly small, perhaps 10 to 20 percent of what would normally be allotted, especially given the incredibly high resident density of these buildings. In effect, these were really dormitories for workers. With a little more effort, and perhaps fewer dwellings and significantly more common space, these could have been an interesting form of living to foster more affordability and community and a broader economic and social mix of residents.

Mietshaeuser Syndikat (Rental House Syndicate)

There is something in the water in Freiburg. The Mietshaeuser Syndikat is a self-organized, tenant-led organization involved in permanently removing housing from the speculative market. Its history is rooted in squatting, beginning with a series of abandoned factory buildings in Freiburg that have since been redeveloped into a thriving community. Each building is intended to be affordable in perpetuity, using cost-based rents instead of market-based rents. Cost-based rent is set at the level needed to repay loans, maintenance, insurance, and taxes.

To prevent groups from leaving the syndicate and pocketing profits, all housing projects are set up as a GmbH (the German version of a limited liability corporation), with both the syndicate and building each having an equal vote. Thus, only with the consent of both parties is it possible to sell or condo-ize a project. The use of the limited liability corporation is an interesting approach: The Syndikat is effectively run as a cooperative, but German laws prevent individual cooperatives from being networked. In order to maximize the effectiveness of the network, an alternative form of governance had to be selected.

For each building, the project's housing association is composed of the tenants of that building, and they are a stakeholder along with the Syndikat. The housing association is responsible for the management, self-governance, rent collection, and financing of their project. There are a variety of paths toward funding projects. The Syndikat brings a level of funding to each project. Direct loans are also used, leaning on the networks of members and those whose ethical or political leanings align with the group. There are currently 190 existing buildings in Germany, with another twenty-one initiatives in planning.[12] Projects range from as few as 4 to as many as 260 residents.

Nearly two thirds of all Syndikat projects in Germany have received financing from GLS Bank.[13] Extensive knowledge is shared between old and new or forming groups. The success of the syndicate is not confined to Germany; the concept has been exported to Switzerland (Genossenschaft Mietshäuser Syndikat), Austria (habiTAT), the Netherlands (VrijCoop), and France (Le Clip). There are occasionally limited opportunities for tenants to buy their homes in the United States, with programs such as Washington, DC's Tenant Opportunity to Purchase Act.[14]

Sufficiency, Connectivity, Flexibility

The Intergovernmental Panel on Climate Change 6th Assessment in 2022 highlighted cohousing and other forms of community-oriented housing as being beneficial in adapting to climate change.[15] Shared amenities allow smaller homes to remain functional and livable, which reduces the consumption of resources during the life of the project and can significantly reduce the embodied carbon of construction. The communal aspects of these projects can also reduce loneliness among elderly residents, children, and parents.

Flexibility is also a central component of these forms of living. Several projects include joker rooms: unprogrammed spaces in the development or building that can be used in a number of ways. A joker room can function as a guest room, providing a shared space for guests to stay so that residents can get by with a smaller and more affordable home. It can function as a teenager's suite, allowing the space for teens to be near, but not necessarily living with, their family. It can function as a caretaker's unit when residents need live-in support services. It can be student housing or short-term rentals to support

the development's economic bottom line. The COVID pandemic showed that the need for spaces for isolation may be important in the future as well. Or it might be just an unprogrammed space that can be used in a variety of ways throughout the day: a music room, a playroom, or a co-working or work-from-home station. The options are almost limitless.

Fostering Housing Diversity

The use of public land allows greater leverage in fostering innovative and affordable housing. Although many cities may be reluctant to use public land for public good, or prevented from doing so by law, fewer policies are more impactful. Vienna, Austria, has been using public land for housing for over a century, including several large mixed-use districts that are predominantly social and nonmarket forms of housing.

The mass timber district in Munich's Prinz-Eugen-Park includes cooperatives, multi-generational Baugruppen, market-rate housing, and social housing. Unit types include maisonettes, flats, and rowhouses, fostering for a multitude of living arrangements. (Credit: Lukas Vallentin)

The German cities of Hamburg, Freiburg, and Tübingen all have land disposition policies related to the use of public land for affordable and middle-class housing. Freiburg's council recently declared that 50 percent of housing in new districts should be affordable rental housing,[16] including social housing, cooperatives, Baugruppen, and rental syndicates. The city will offer affordable land for these initiatives. Federal states and cities, such as Berlin, also publish reports[17] on what types of collective housing are formed and financed, often with built examples.

Hamburg's Agentur für Baugemeinschaften (Department for Building Communities; *Baugemeinschaften* is similar in meaning to *Baugruppen*) has been in operation since 2003[18] and fulfills a number of functions. The department connects people looking for building groups. It provides guidance on administrative requirements; connects groups with potential architects, builders, and financing; and even deals with property disposition and tendering. One of the more intriguing aspects of land disposition is the city's stated goal of reserving 20 percent of land released for development for Baugruppen. When the city offers land and multiple building groups apply, a selection process ensues. It is the city's approach to fostering more innovation: The option to purchase the land (usually at or near cost) is awarded to the group with the best concept, with evaluations based on social diversity, sustainability, affordability, feasibility, and inclusion. The team with the winning concept then has one year to finalize building permits and line up financing. Since its inception, the department has overseen 3,300 new homes, with another 1,400 in planning and construction.

Amsterdam owns 80 percent of the land within the city limits,[19] with most housing and buildings operating under a ground lease. This allows the city sizable leverage in using its land for community- and value-oriented projects. The city has committed that by 2045, 10 percent of all homes in Amsterdam will be cooperatives. To promote this goal, the city has a €50 million loan fund for gap financing and will be periodically releasing land for housing cooperatives.[20]

The leadership these cities have shown toward fostering new forms of living elevates the discussion at regional, national, and even international levels. This can be seen where even small villages in Germany have taken up the mantle of prioritizing Baugruppen and other forms of nonmarket housing in their districts and developing neighborhoods.

Cities are realizing that diverse and affordable housing is a net gain, and prioritizing policies to allow working- and middle-class households to stay in their community makes for better cities. Because of the value-oriented nature of the development, it also tends to be more ecologically sustainable and generally of higher quality than market-driven development. Construction and neighborhood reintensification mean more jobs in the city. Stronger communities are fostered. The city's tax base is also increased because these households don't decamp for the suburbs. This is the power of a values-driven proposition instead of a profit-motivated one.

CHAPTER 12

Child-Friendly Districts

"Children are a kind of indicator species. If we can build a successful city for children, we will have a successful city for all people."

—Enrique Peñalosa, former mayor of Bogotá, Colombia

Families want to live in walkable urban neighborhoods—close to schools, close to transportation, with high-quality public space, natural areas, and daily needs nearby. Yet building regulations severely limit the viability and livability of family-friendly dwellings in new multifamily buildings and transit-oriented development (TOD). New housing around TOD tends to

A typical three-bedroom dwelling in a point access block allows for a similar quality of life as detached houses or rowhouses: light on multiple sides, the ability to cross-ventilate, and separate living and sleeping areas. It is rare that three-bedroom apartments in new US construction offer similar qualities, largely because of anomalous building codes. (Credit: Michael Eliason/Larch Lab)

be quite large and lacks the amenities or spaces that families might prefer, such as playrooms, music rooms, or large storage areas for strollers and cargo bikes. According to the Harvard Joint Center for Housing Studies, families with children are more than twice as likely to be found in buildings with two to nineteen dwellings,[1] perhaps revealing a preference for smaller buildings.

TOD lacks the quiet streets and the abundance of public and green spaces found in child-friendly ecodistricts such as Seestadt and Vauban. In an *Atlantic* article, architecture and design critic Alexandra Lange describes a number of ways family life could be improved in cities: "Slow down cars, narrow streets, add more trees, especially in shade deserts. Placing family-oriented venues close together would help create easy routes between them—and it might allow them to feed off one another. If a child can safely run around at a nearby playground while their parent does an exercise class at the community center, for example, then there's no need to hire a babysitter."[2] It is noteworthy that all of those elements are the exact things found in ecodistricts!

Like many other European cities, Vienna aims to provide both programmed and unprogrammed space for kids and teens. During district planning, they even engage with youth to find out what their needs are. US cities should follow suit. (Credit: Mark Ostrow)

102 Building for People

Where Did All the Family-Sized Homes Go?

The demographic inversion of the post–Baby Boom era and the corresponding dropoff in new multifamily housing built between the 1980s and 2000s can be seen in the vastness of the overlapping crises in the United States. Housing shortages in urban areas are causing rampant price increases. Inadequate affordable housing is causing economic displacement and herculean commutes. Baby Boomers who bought when prices in urban areas were incredibly low find they can't move because most of their wealth is locked up in their homes, and new housing near them is incredibly expensive. Families are locked out of the housing market, refusing to deal with herculean commutes in unwalkable neighborhoods and crowding into small apartments. (See Chapter 11 on housing types.)

It isn't just a shortage in the *number* of dwellings but in the *types* of dwellings. In 2022 multifamily housing starts reached levels last seen in the late 1980s. Yet there are 30 percent more households today than there were in 1988. There is a distinct lack of family-sized homes, especially affordable ones in multifamily buildings in US cities. This deficit is even more noticeable in TOD: A 2015 Census Working Paper revealed that between 2006 and 2013, both in and around Washington, DC, blocks within a half-mile of a rail station saw the percentage of six to seventeen-year-old residents decrease, even as children under six years of age increased.[3] Increasingly, TOD and station areas are marketed and planned for singles, couples without children, and empty nesters.

According to a report by the Zürcher Kantonalbank, nearly one third of all homes built in Zurich in 2022 consisted of three or more bedrooms.[4] Vancouver encourages grouping family-sized apartments on the same floor to encourage social contact and avoid complaints about noise.[5]

This is a stark contrast to US urban development: Just 2 percent of apartments in Seattle have three or more bedrooms.[6] A recent San Francisco Planning Department report noted that only 30 percent of three-bedroom dwellings were occupied by families with children.[7]

Because of the economics of construction and the peculiarities of the US building code that prevent midrise point access blocks, there is a sizable disincentive to create affordable and livable family-sized homes in multifamily housing. These typically limit three-bedroom dwellings to the corners of buildings, reducing the number of family-sized homes in midrise buildings. Because US apartments tend to be much larger than in other countries, developers plan these homes for roommates rather than families, with three-bedroom dwellings having three (or even more) bathrooms. Apartments tend to have bedrooms of the same size, rather than having larger bedrooms for parents and smaller bedrooms for children, as is typical in Europe. Stephen Smith at the Center for Building in North America notes, "American plans have significantly more floor area for the same number of bedrooms, and have much more lightless interior space up against the common corridor to fill—inevitably with bathrooms, closets, and larger kitchens. For families—which tend to be inherently more financially strapped than singles, childless couples, or roommates, since they're likely to have kids, older adults, and even parents who aren't working in the household—the cost of all this extra square footage can be too much to bear."[8]

Cities try to incentivize the production of larger family-sized homes through a variety of tools—height increases, floor area ratio bonuses or exemptions (increases in allowed building area, or exemption of floor area, for including family-sized homes)—but these are all largely irrelevant when floor area ratio and allowed lot coverage are already high compared with those in other countries. As indicated in Chapter 6, the path to more family-sized homes—not just in ecodistricts but in all development—will require rethinking how we build in the US. Our codes need to shift dramatically to promote the diversity and larger dwellings found in other countries, even in small buildings. Our financing regimes need to adapt so that families and multigenerational households aren't locked out of living in walkable neighborhoods, so a broad economic mix of families can live in walkable areas. Perhaps the largest area for improvement is for federal and state policies to better align the needs of families and opportunities for low-carbon living.

Daycare and Multifunctional Schools

Most TOD in the United States does not include new school construction, and often even daycare facilities are left to the whims of the market. This isn't the case in other countries, where schools are integrated into larger districts and daycare facilities are concurrently planned. New schools can draw in families, and because districts are planned with more than a token handful of family-sized homes, they get used.

Schools in the ecodistrict can be planned as collated educational campuses, as in the case of Sonnwendviertel, where daycare, primary school, middle, and even secondary school are collated. Educational facilities can also be distributed throughout the district, as in the case of Oberbillwerder, with daycare and primary schools distributed in the distinct neighborhoods and the secondary campus central to the mobility hub and commercial core of the district.

When schools are integrated with TOD planning, opportunities emerge for the shared use of gyms, libraries, auditoriums, and sports fields between education facilities. They can also serve as shared public amenities, offering extracurricular activities outside school. Auditoriums and gymnasiums can be used for neighborhood purposes. The proximity of the mixed-use

When I first visited Vienna's Nordbahnhof, I was floored that this neighborhood full of family-friendly multifamily housing and Baugruppen was quieter than the single-family neighborhood we lived in. The number of children present far exceeded any near our home in Seattle. (Credit: Lukasz Karnas)

district also allows it to become a sort of laboratory for middle and secondary schools, offering extracurricular learning locations or perhaps exposing young adults to potential career paths in the productive city. In Berlin, adult education facilities are also being co-located with schools, turning them into places of learning for all.

Parks and Open Spaces (Car-Free Spaces) Nearby

In Freiburg's Vauban, car-free streets enable safe and quick cycling or walking to transit in order to get to school, daycare, or activities in the city and region. Vienna's Sonnwendviertel operates in a similar manner, and most

Child-Friendly Districts 105

children living in the district can get to its educational campus without crossing a single street. Hamburg's Oberbillwerder ecodistrict features a green loop circumnavigating the district's neighborhoods and connecting to schools, daycares, parks, and social and cultural spaces. This car-free loop allows parents or children to walk or bike to these places without having to interact with traffic.

Making cities more attractive for families to live and work is often a stated goal in comprehensive plans. Without changes, the way we plan our cities is largely at odds with those aims. For children today, ecodistricts allow the types of spaces and lifestyle I was able to have as a child: with freedom to roam, accessible and unstructured. Having places where it is safe to walk, that are convenient for those with strollers, also makes it more accessible to people with disabilities and the elderly. Ultimately, ecodistricts offer the potential of gaining back the hundreds of hours that parents waste commuting every year, driving to run simple errands that could easily be accomplished in walkable places. Prioritizing such places would mean more time with the family. More time with friends. More time to explore, to play, or to just be. One need only look at the success of groups working to make better cities, in the United States and elsewhere, with school streets, open streets, café streets, and the walking and bike bus movements, to see that there is a significant need and a demand for these kinds of spaces.

CHAPTER 13

Air and Noise Pollution

Much of the transit-oriented development (TOD) and station area development in the United States is centered on heavily congested arterials (rather than being located adjacent to them) or bounded by them. In some instances, high-capacity transit lines are positioned alongside, or even in the median, of a highway, reducing the amount of developable land around stations. This is true for many systems currently expanding, including Seattle's Sound Transit, Phoenix, Denver, and WMATA's expansion in the Washington, DC, metro. The political reasoning behind this approach, one intended as a path of least resistance with as little change as possible, is understandable. But it makes development more challenging from a geometric and economic standpoint. More importantly, from a public health and livability perspective, it is an incredibly problematic approach to planning.

Furthermore, there is a pernicious myth that density must be noisy. As *The War on Cars* podcaster Doug Gordon has noted, "Cities aren't loud, cars are

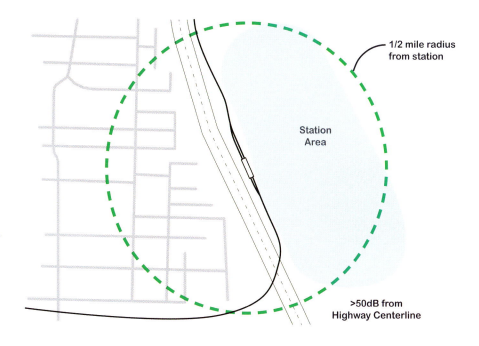

US land use policies tend to position transit-oriented development stations alongside or even in the middle of highways, putting most of the dense housing in an area where air and noise pollution (red) are highest. Unfortunately, electric vehicles do not solve this problem. (Credit: Michael Eliason/ Larch Lab)

Air and Noise Pollution 107

loud."[1] The quietness of Freiburg's car-free Altstadt had a profound effect on my understanding of urban noise and noise pollution. Its nearly car-free district of Vauban offers a similar take on how quiet urban areas can be, even outside the city core. During the pandemic lockdown, we found our neighborhood to be so quiet and serene in ways we never thought possible, an effect that the *New York Times* noted was widespread.[2] On a recent trip to Tokyo, my entire family was awestruck by how quiet a car-light city of nearly fourteen million residents could be. We could sleep with the windows open, and it was quieter on the sixth floor in a district largely composed of midrise and high-rise buildings than the accessory dwelling unit in the Seattle single-family neighborhood where we reside. Children could be heard laughing and running to school as we got ready for the day. Having right-sized vehicles for urban areas, an accessible and comprehensive transit system, and a culture of widespread cycling for all ages and abilities results in far fewer cars on the road, leading to less noise pollution and quieter, more livable cities. Paris deputy mayor David Belliard declared, "Too much noise makes people sick," and the city turned to ticketing drivers of noisy vehicles to reduce noise pollution.[3] Directly addressing the harm caused by car-induced noise pollution has significant co-benefits and positive public health outcomes that cities serious about livability, safe streets, and climate action should be prioritizing.

The negative public health effects of air and noise pollution have been known for decades. Every year there are more and more data to bolster the findings that building housing near toxic arterials is, as policy analyst Daniel Oleksiuk calls it, "a devil's bargain."[4] Time and time again, this is exactly where jurisdictions decide to focus new and affordable multifamily housing. Current planning trends look to double down on this by largely limiting rezones directly on major arterials and boulevards.[5] These arterials are typically four- to six-lane roads, some with center-running transit, and pedestrian-oriented sidewalks and bike lanes at the edges. Again, it seems to be an approach that takes the path of least resistance rather than one that is guided by public health and user experience. From a livability standpoint, focusing so many residents who have no ability to escape the air and noise pollution, and requiring them to constantly cross 100-foot-wide (or wider!) streetscapes to reach transit or run errands, shows little concern for their time, safety, or quality of life. Seattle's own experiment limiting density along a four-lane arterial with center-running transit has been a costly disaster, with numerous accidents, fatalities, and transit delays.[6]

Government agencies often play up the environmental benefits of TOD: reduced greenhouse gas emissions, improved air quality with increased transit usage, and even reductions in microplastics from reduced car usage. Although these

Pedestrian zones, low-traffic neighborhoods, and car-free streets like those shown in this neighborhood in Tokyo's Asakusa not only are more enjoyable places to live but also have better public health outcomes. (Credit: Michael Eliason)

are true on a regional scale, focusing new density along the most toxic and dangerous streets is a policy that puts those residents directly in harm's way. This is especially problematic from an equity standpoint, because the majority of residents in TOD are renters who cannot afford expensive homes in quieter neighborhoods with cleaner air. In addition, as with all things urban planning in the United States, there are significant racial and socioeconomic impacts of air pollution exposure.[7]

Long-term exposure to air pollution from traffic is associated with lung cancer.[8] Prolonged air pollution is associated with a number of chronic health conditions, including cardiovascular disease, stroke, asthma, chronic obstructive pulmonary disease, diabetes, and mental health conditions. The effects of air pollution are also amplified by extreme heat and climate change. The Environmental Protection Agency (EPA) Fourth National Climate Assessment warns, "Unless counteracting efforts to improve air quality are implemented,

Moderate and high levels of density pair well with low-traffic streets, like this one in Munich's Theresienpark residential district. The district is planned so that noise levels at night are not bothersome. (Credit: Michael Eliason)

climate change will worsen existing air pollution levels. This worsened air pollution would increase the incidence of adverse respiratory and cardiovascular health effects, including premature death."[9]

As with air pollution, noise pollution is more than just a nuisance. Chronic exposure to noise pollution is associated with a number of health conditions, including annoyance, sleep disturbance, and cardiovascular issues such as hypertension.[10] A 2021 study in Denmark noted, "Transportation noise from road traffic and railway [is] associated with increased risk of all cause dementia and dementia subtypes, especially Alzheimer's disease."[11] Knowing all this, it is perplexing that there is no course of action to address either of these issues at federal or state level.

Regulating Noise

Although there is air pollution regulation, albeit irregularly enforced, there is no US legislation regulating noise pollution or enforcing noise control. The EPA's own website states,

> In the 1970s, EPA coordinated all federal noise control activities through its Office of Noise Abatement and Control. EPA phased out the office's funding in 1982 as part of a shift in federal noise control policy to transfer the primary responsibility of regulating noise to state and local governments. However, the Noise Control Act of 1972 and the Quiet Communities Act of 1978 were never rescinded by Congress and remain in effect today, although they are essentially unfunded.[12]

In 2021, a congressional bill to fund and update the 1978 Quiet Communities Act was filed,[13] with the stated goal of reestablishing the Office of Noise Abatement and Control within the EPA. It did not make it out of committee.

It is noteworthy that although jurisdictions refuse to regulate or measure noise pollution, the US Department of Housing and Urban Development (HUD) does, to a limited extent, regulate it. Notably, the language in HUD Noise Standards[14] uses the term *goals*, and HUD's General Acceptability Standard[15] allows a day–night average sound level (L_{dn}, the average noise level over a twenty-four-hour period) to reach 65 decibels. This standard imposes a 10-decibel penalty on noise emitted between 10 p.m. and 7 a.m. The European Union uses the day–evening–night noise level (L_{den}), a subtle difference that imposes a 5-decibel penalty on noise from 7 p.m. to 10 p.m. and a 10-decibel penalty on noise emitted from 10 p.m. to 7 a.m. Generally, these are similar results; however, the weighting of Lden used in the European Union is a slightly stricter standard and captures more of the nuisance of louder noise pollution generated in urban areas at night.

Comparatively, the European Union and its member states are much more proactive on the issue of noise pollution. The EU's Environmental Noise Directive[16] requires member countries to prepare and publish noise maps and noise management action plans every five years for medium and large cities. These maps are drawn to indicate noise levels at the façade of buildings, so there's a much broader sense of granularity to them. Although the European Union does not regulate noise pollution, it does set up a framework for member states to monitor and mitigate it independently. Not quite a panacea, but it is significant improvement that US cities would be wise to adopt.

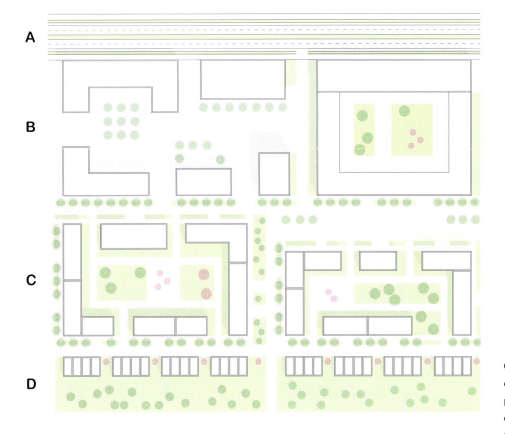

One approach used in several ecodistricts to mitigate noise pollution is layering commercial and mixed-use buildings (B), directly on the arterial (A), with building forms that limit noise propagation to residential areas and open space (C), or off the arterial, allowing for quiet and peaceful parks and open space (D). (Credit: Michael Eliason/Larch Lab)

Lessening Noise for Livability

Some of the measures implemented to reduce noise pollution in European cities include burying roads, building noise barriers, imposing traffic restrictions such as pedestrian zones or low-traffic networks, introducing 20-mile-per-hour speed zones (and lower), promoting alternative modes of

As in Vienna's Sonnwendviertel, where density is located off major roads, districts can be planned so that they do not have cut through traffic or streets where speeding is the norm. This not only reduces noise pollution for residents but also makes for safer neighborhoods. (Credit: Albert Koch)

transportation, and soundproofing buildings through additional levels of insulation and noise-mitigating windows. Paris under mayor Anne Hidalgo has been a leader in livability and the connection to safe streets, air pollution, and noise pollution. Over the last few years, Paris has waged a war on noise pollution by closing down streets to cars, adding bike lanes throughout the city, and targeting noisy vehicles.[17] German planning guidelines in the federal Traffic Noise Protection Ordinance[18] indicate a nighttime maximum of 49 decibels for the allgemeine Wohngebeiete, general residential areas found in urban environments, or 54 decibels for the core or mixed urban areas. When it comes to noise protection and the urban planning of districts, DIN 18005-1 Sound Insulation in Urban Planning[19] lays out guidelines for planning new districts to ensure a high quality of life and less disruption. Those guidelines are a nighttime maximum of 45 decibels for general residential areas and 50 decibels for denser core and mixed-use urban areas. This norm also includes a table indicating the distance to be maintained from the center of the traffic route *without* noise protection measures, and with line of sight, in order not to exceed required noise levels. The *minimum* distance for not exceeding the 50-decibel threshold at night is 1,300 meters (4,265 feet) from the highway and 70 meters (230 feet) from the center of major arterials. It should be noted that 230 feet is nearly the width of a full block in most US cities—and the very place most dense multifamily housing is limited to.

The fairly extensive noise modeling informs EU cities where hotspots are so that they can be addressed and allows planning teams to ensure that new ecodistricts are not inundated by noise pollution. There are several options planning teams can incorporate to mitigate noise pollution at the neighborhood and district scale. The strongest approach is source control, which is accomplished largely with the construction of noise barriers or berms to reduce noise and line-of-sight issues or positioning the district at a distance away from the source.

District-Scale Solutions

Planning at the district scale usually begins with the goal of noise-resistant structures, for creating quiet areas and urban compatibility. This can be done through a number of strategies, including closed building forms, the incorporation of a noise barrier or wall, co-locating urban development based on noise compatibility, and other measures. Occasionally, this does mean there are glazed noise walls spanning between buildings; my feelings on this are mixed. After living in Germany, I miss the quiet found in dense areas, a sense that is largely nonexistent in US cities.

Another possibility is use-based layering of buildings, which admittedly is one of my favorite solutions. This entails positioning uses where more noise exposure is acceptable (retail, commercial, workshops, offices, hotels, student housing) directly on or near the arterial, rails, or source of noise, followed by another layer or layers of residential buildings in the quieter zones behind it. This was the strategy for the winning entry by bauchplan and ISSS research–architecture–urbanism for Regensburg's Prince Leopold and Pioneer Barracks planning competition, which places the park at the literal heart and quietest part of the site, surrounded by residential buildings, and then businesses, commercial, mixed use, and garages along the arterials and railyard that bound the site.

Block-Scale Solution

The urban form also has subtle effects on air and noise pollution. An informative paper presented at the 2019 International Seminar on Urban Form looked at the effects of air and noise pollution for urban forms such as the closed perimeter block to towers in the park. It concluded, "Types that reduce noise exposure in the [court] yards, increase air pollution on the sidewalks and vice versa, types that reduce concentration of nitrogen oxides on the sidewalk, increase noise exposure in the yards."[20] Unsurprisingly, closed perimeter blocks have quiet courtyards, but air pollution emissions end up being concentrated on the sidewalks, which makes sense as the air pollution becomes trapped on the streets. Semipermeable L-shaped blocks with open corners still block the sound well but allow more mixing of the air to

Closed building forms along arterials can block noise pollution, allowing for quiet inner streets and courtyards, as in Vienna's Sonnwendviertel. (Credit: Albert Koch)

dilute air pollution. A follow-up study conducted by the same team, looking at intensification of existing blocks, found similar results and determined that varying building heights on closed or semipermeable perimeter blocks allowed better mixing of air to deal with air pollution while reducing noise pollution.[21] This height variability at the block scale is accomplished only with regulations allowing taller point access blocks.

The issues of urban form and morphology are not talked about enough in the United States and Canada, nor are their effects on air pollution, noise pollution, and mitigating overheating. All these problems are further compounded where the preponderance of double-loaded corridors prevents any mitigation of these issues. This is just one more reason code reform needs to be a priority. These are also problems to mitigate in existing districts. The recompaction and reintensification of existing blocks and neighborhoods, and retrofitting for better social-ecological outcomes, also entails significant work.

Building-Scale Solution

Buildings themselves can also be noise barriers. One approach that is fairly common in EU districts is to position commercial or mixed-use buildings continuously along the arterial (use-based layering), filtering to residential

Air and Noise Pollution 115

development set off internally from that. Whether it is opened or closed, the building form also plays a role in noise mitigation. The continuous nature of closed buildings blocks noise.

At the building level, there are still further paths to reducing noise pollution. Building form and even dwelling access can offer noise protection. Because the building itself acts as a noise barrier, placing bedrooms on the nonarterial side of the building increases noise protection for sleeping residents. This is one of the many great things about point access blocks discussed in Chapter 5: Often, the bedrooms can be positioned on the quiet side of the building. In typical development in the United States, consisting of the hotel-like double-loaded corridor, dwellings on the street do not have the ability to block the noise. Residents who live directly on loud, noxious streets are forced to live with a multitude of negative public health effects.

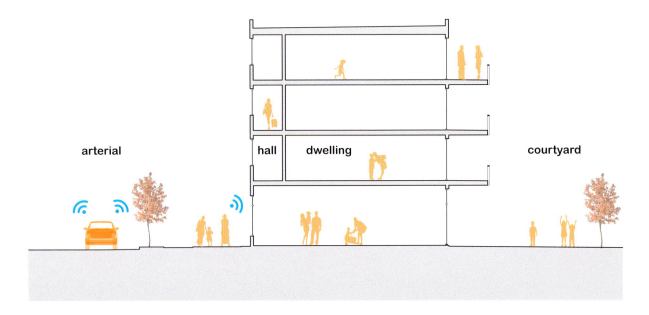

Single-loaded corridors can be designed so that the access corridors are positioned along the road, with dwellings and bedrooms placed on the quiet courtyard side of the building. Another step for increasing noise protection in single-loaded corridors is to enclose the corridor, providing a conditioned or semiconditioned buffer from the street and living space.

This is also an area where the many co-benefits of the Passive House standard from Chapter 16 are noticeable. The airtight construction, thermal bridge–free detailing, and continuous optimal insulation levels reduce noise from entering the building. The triple-pane windows also can play a role in increasing noise protection. One of the more impressive examples of this is

Single-loaded corridors can be positioned so that the accessway is enclosed, using the hallway as a buffer between the street and the dwellings. This places the focus of the dwellings on the quieter, rear courtyard. (Credit: Michael Eliason/Larch Lab)

Treberspurg & Partner Architekten's Passive House social housing complex on Vienna's Kaisermuehlenstrasse.[22] The complex is located with a highway, shunting yard, and above-grade U-Bahn station within a quarter mile of the development. A long, continuous single-loaded corridor is positioned to block the noise, with all dwellings opening up on to the quiet side of the building. The enclosed corridor and Passive House detailing ensure that even the corridor is not loud while passing through. The balance of the development consists of free-standing point access blocks arranged perpendicular to the sound-deflecting single-loaded corridor. I visited during the Passive House conference in 2017. I was amazed at how quiet the lush interior of this development was; the sounds of birds and children laughing in contrast to the incredible noise pollution from cars and rails just beyond was life altering.

Urban noise is a major public health issue that has serious effects on livability and quality of life. However, noise pollution does not have to be omnipresent in cities. Tokyo, a city of nearly fourteen million residents, is one of the quietest cities I have ever been to, with dense areas being significantly less noisy than the single-family neighborhood in Seattle where we live. Cities tackling noise pollution will find they are at the forefront of issues of livability and public health. Ecodistricts can play an important role in helping shape noise policy and mitigating noise pollution within the district.

PART III

Climate Adaptation and Nature

120 Building for People

CHAPTER 14

Green Space

Top, Vienna's Nordbahnhof neighborhood is centered on the 7.6-acre Rudolf Bednar Park. When you're standing in the middle, it's hard to tell the park is surrounded by seven- to ten-story buildings. The park features areas for sports, play, and respite. (Credit: Lukasz Karnas)

Left, In the middle of Munich's Domagpark, a massive park features a large area for stormwater mitigation, with a play structure highlighting the topography. (Credit: Friedrich Ludewig)

There are many reasons that an ecodistrict should have an abundance of open and green space: to have adequate space to get around, to play, to meet, and to have social gatherings. These spaces are also necessary to mitigate and adapt to the effects of climate change. Trees and abundant green space can mitigate the urban heat island effect. Parks can double as stormwater retention.

Access to nature is associated with numerous mental, social, and physical benefits and co-benefits. Proximity to nature and spaces to recreate or socialize outdoors increases physical activity. In urban areas they are especially beneficial to the mental and physical health of at-risk people, including the elderly and children.[1] Green spaces can allow informal gathering, and they can strengthen social ties in the district and surrounding areas.

The World Health Organization states that "urban green space is a necessary component for delivering healthy, sustainable and liveable cities."[2] There is ample research showing that being closer to parks and natural areas in urban settings correlates with improved well-being and levels of happiness.[3] One of the largest differentiators between transit-oriented development and ecodistricts is the amount of vegetated and car-free space found in the latter. This is partially related to thinner buildings, allowing for more green and open space at the block level, but also to the incorporation of significantly larger parks.

In many US cities, there is inequitable access to parks and open space for a number of reasons, and larger parks are located predominantly in wealthier and whiter neighborhoods.[4] The World Health Organization recommends that residents have access to "at least one acre of public green space within 300 meters of their homes."[5] Proximity is a significant factor in the use of parks and open space, and this is where the park-centered planning of the ecodistrict excels. A 2005 study on parks and proximity concluded, "Good access to attractive and large POS [public open space] is associated with higher levels of walking."[6] Close proximity is also correlated with higher

numbers of visits to parks and duration of visits.[7] Abundant car-free and car-light ways around the ecodistrict, and large parks and near-direct access, make walking and rolling an easy choice.

Parks and natural areas can serve as buffers, both physical and visual. These buffers can also dampen environmental noise pollution, creating a better environment within the ecodistrict. A 16-foot heavily vegetated tree stand can reduce noise pollution from traffic by 9 to 11 decibels.[8] The visual power of nature is also strong, and just the presence of it may have the functional effect of reducing noise pollution by 10 decibels.[9]

Natural areas provide abundant space for increasing biodiversity in urban areas. Forests integrated into the district provide space for flora, fauna, and climate mitigation through reduced heat islands. They can also offer shinrin-yoku, forest bathing, a practice conceived in Japan to help people reconnect with nature while decreasing levels of stress and burnout. Forest bathing also is associated with mental and cardiovascular benefits.[10] Berlin's Schumacher Quartier will prioritize biodiversity from the outset, targeting the introduction of fourteen animal species with the appropriate habitats where they can thrive,[11] through animal-aided design, "a methodology that reconciles wildlife conservation and urban design at the local scale. . . . The

The park-oriented ecodistrict offers a quality of living that is as high as, or higher than, living in single-family neighborhoods. The soft edges of Hammarby Sjöstad in Stockholm, Sweden, allow the interstitial space between dense blocks and the water to be publicly accessible. (Credit: Alex Linthicum)

basic idea of Animal-Aided Design is to include the presence of animals in the planning process, such that they become an integral part of the design."[12]

Ecodistricts incorporate programmed green spaces, including various community gardens, orchards, and pea patches. Playgrounds and places for teens and young adults to play or gather are integral to nearly every ecodistrict I have visited. Playgrounds can be located in semipublic courtyards or interspersed throughout the district. Sports fields are normally co-located with schools and educational campuses, for use by the schools during the day. They can also be used by the larger community outside school hours.

Courtyards are common in ecodistricts, and because of their significantly thinner buildings, they are typically much larger than courtyards in the United States. Even within a courtyard, there are a number of decisions to be made about public and private space. Is the courtyard private? Are there private terraces directly adjacent to the building, with a larger common area in the middle? Is the courtyard accessible to the public? Courtyards can vary from private ones in closed perimeter blocks accessible only to residents and guests to semipublic courtyards in semipermeable perimeter blocks. This is an arrangement I find particularly beneficial, because it allows for increased levels of daylight and views while allowing airflow. The semipermeable

Trees can increase visual and acoustic separation between dwellings and public pathways, as in this car-free stretch of Seestadt in Vienna. (Credit: Mark Ostrow)

Top, Sonnwendviertel's 17-acre Helmut-Zilk-Park is located in the middle of the district, connecting the various sections while providing abundant open and green space for residents in both the ecodistrict and surrounding neighborhoods. (Credit: Albert Koch)

Left, Private outdoor spaces including balconies, loggia, and terraces can offer great places to view urban life, especially when located away from loud arterials. (Credit: Michael Eliason)

perimeter block feels more closed off than it is, and so it does provide a visual separation, without a physical barrier.

Private Outdoor Space

As with public and semipublic spaces, there should also be a broad variety of private outdoor spaces. Ground floor apartments and maisonettes can have private terraces at grade—a great option for families. These spaces do not need to be very large; even 10 to 15 feet would suffice. Typically, some sort of treatment establishes this zone as private space, as opposed to public or semipublic.

Balconies should be deep enough for at least a small table and chair. Large and functional cantilevered balconies are much more common in European and South American cities. Balconies can perform multiple duties, acting as sun protection or even deflecting urban noise. There are climate implications for balconies. They should be thermally broken to ensure greater durability and resident comfort. A thermal break is a material inserted between two materials to reduce cold bridging and associated heat loss, which reduces mold risk as well. Deluges and cloudbursts can lead to flooding if there is inadequate separation or drainage.

Loggia are semiprotected outdoor rooms with openings on one or two sides, like an inset porch. They offer a private outdoor space and are generally more protected from the elements than balconies. From a climate standpoint, heavy rains can be problematic. One solution might be to have operable shutters or winter garden glazing that can be closed to block out the elements.

Roof decks and terraces have become quite common in US housing in recent years. Although they can be great private outdoor spaces, I have serious concerns about how they hold up to severe climate events as cloudbursts drop far more water than roof drains or scuppers were designed for. A better function of roofscapes is for stormwater mitigation; blue roofs can double as spaces for urban gardening or energy production with photovoltaic panels.

The soundscapes of ecodistricts are quite fascinating. Districts that take noise pollution into account, using natural or physical buffers in addition to urban forms that drastically reduce noise pollution, allow for incredibly quiet places despite a moderate or even high population density. Freiburg's Vauban is incredibly quiet; you can readily hear children playing. At Rieselfeld and Muenchen-Riem, the sounds of birds singing are prominent and delightful (my mother is an avid birder, so it's hard not to notice these things). Although there is little data, the soundscapes of ecodistricts—with parks,

green spaces, and a moderate level of density—are probably much quieter than the majority of transit-oriented development, situated along or adjacent to arterials and highways, with little noise mitigation.

As we saw during the pandemic, having the ability to get outside (whether in a private space, parks, or car-free streets)—the ability to commune with one another, to enjoy nature, to get outside and walk about socially distanced—was imperative for mental health[13] and also for physical activity and health. These health effects show a massive improvement over the effects of living in sprawling areas and may help counteract sedentary lifestyles therein.[14] Ecodistricts also better position cities to meet the priorities of the European Union's Green City Accord: air quality, water, biodiversity, waste, and noise.[15]

Districts that offer a multitude of outdoor environments for everyday living, with buildings that do the same, will be better positioned to handle the various curveballs climate change will deliver. Flexible spaces, which offer connections to nature and climate adaptation measures, allow for numerous benefits and should be the focus of districts offering a high quality of life.

A semipublic courtyard in Vienna's Seestadt offers a level of accessible quietness that is rare in arterial or highway-adjacent developments. (Credit: Lukasz Karnas)

CHAPTER 15

Sponge Cities and Water Loops

"Whether it's managed retreat, de-development, depaving, ripping out, tearing up, a lot of intentional design in the future will be about the action of unmaking—taking concrete out of water bodies, jackhammering and removing roads from critical migration paths, densifying the high ground, or softening watery edges."

—Kate Orff

Climate change is full of contradictions, causing enduring drought over long periods of time and then dropping enormous volumes of rain over a very short period of time, followed again by drought. Extreme weather events have increased significantly since 1970.[1] Floods were the most frequent disaster worldwide from 2000 to 2014, leading to over 85,000 deaths and significant damage.[2] With climate change, this will probably worsen, and cities will need to find ways to rapidly adapt to significant storm and flooding events. The ecodistrict allows for a multitude of nature-based solutions (NBSs) to address these events. This is where the green nature of ecodistricts excels.

The World Bank defines NBSs as "actions to protect, sustainably manage and restore natural and modified ecosystems in ways that address societal challenges effectively and adaptively, to provide both human well-being and biodiversity benefits."[3] Planning for storm and flood events is easier at larger scales, with UN Habitat noting that the economies of scale of urbanization and cities "make it cheaper and easier to take actions to minimize both emissions and climate hazards."[4] NBSs in ecodistricts can include biodiversity corridors, adaptation and mitigation solutions for climate change, urban heat island mitigation and natural cooling, and stormwater adaptation. One of the most effective approaches for existing neighborhoods or brownfields is depaving[5] and unsealing paved surfaces. In the ecodistrict, sealed surfaces and paving should be minimized.

Cities and flooding will increasingly become intertwined, and cities will need to rethink their relationship with both stormwater and floods. Professor Kuei-Hsien Liao notes that with a "shift in perception and creative planning and design, cities can eventually phase out flood-control infrastructure and live with floods by retrofitting the built environment and adding redundancy, diversity, and flexibility into every subsystem."[6]

Water management is increasingly crucial to development, and districts should have a multitude of approaches to dealing with increased rainfall. This should entail storage and retention across a variety of surfaces. In addition, a district's public open space, green spaces, and even sports fields can offer potential solutions. In Munich's Domagkpark, the playground is situated in a large recess that doubles as stormwater retention. In Hamburg's Oberbillwerder ecodistrict, currently in planning, the Green Loop, the recreational car-free path navigating the district, will function as storage capacity for hundred-year rain events.[7]

Flood risks should be accounted for, and cities should avoid development in hundred-year floodplains. The potential for flooding subterranean dwellings should also be evaluated when planning housing for the district. Hurricane Ida in New York City led to eleven people drowning in basement apartments,[8] and for that reason I will never work on an underground accessory dwelling unit again.

The pedestrian and bike paths around the climate adaptive park at the heart of Domagpark in Munich are not paved, allowing greater permeability than concrete or asphalt while reducing reflectivity and the urban heat island effect. (Credit: Friedrich Ludewig)

128 Building for People

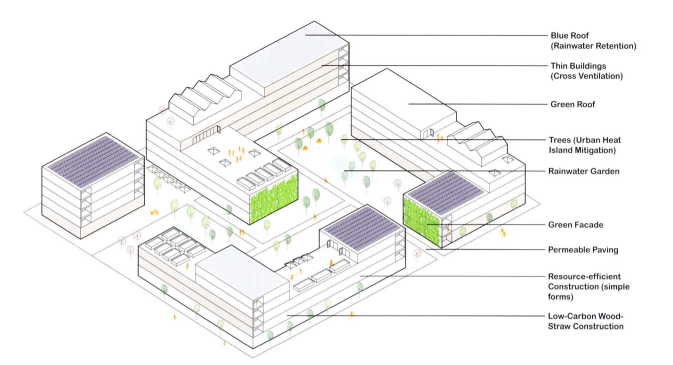

Sponge Cities

The sponge city is an urban planning concept oriented around flood and stormwater management associated with green infrastructure. The concept originated in China and has been heavily adopted in German cities and increasingly in US cities such as Pittsburgh and Los Angeles.[9] In the United States, in the wake of previous flooding events and to mitigate future deluges and rain events, cities such as New York are beginning to adopt sponge city principles.

Sponge city strategies at the district level can include subsoil storage, depending on soil conditions; parks and other large green areas such as medians, shared gardens, and tree wells; streetscapes through bioswales or pervious paving; small-scale soft spaces such as private courtyards, private gardens, and the green space around buildings in the ecodistrict; and blue roofs on buildings.

Floodable open spaces, such as those in Domagkpark and Oberbillwerder, do not just offer the direct benefit of detaining stormwater. They also provide numerous co-benefits: improved air quality, carbon sequestration,[10] spaces for recreation and physical activity, places to congregate and socialize, and space for biodiversity.

Urban heat islands can be mitigated through parks and open space and through larger courtyards behind buildings in the ecodistrict. Shade and evapotranspiration reduce peak air temperatures during heat events.[11]

Blocks with thinner and taller buildings, such as point access blocks, allow for significantly more blue-green infrastructure, including stormwater mitigation and space for trees to reduce the urban heat island effect. They also increase privacy for residents. (Credit: Michael Eliason/Larch Lab)

Circular Water

Water scarcity is becoming worse. All over the southwestern United States, cities are facing long and severe droughts affecting water availability. According to a 2016 study, "Two-thirds of the global population (4.0 billion people) live under conditions of severe water scarcity at least 1 month of the year."[12] At the same time, growing cities are consuming more water. As with the production of carbon emissions, the wealthy use a disproportionate amount of water resources, with a study showing that the nonessential use of water by wealthy residents is a growing problem.[13] The idea of sufficiency as it relates to climate adaptation and resilience means reducing the consumption of resources including energy, carbon, and water to live within planetary boundaries while not compromising quality of life. In addition to reducing water consumption, more efforts are needed in reusing water resources.

Closing the water loops, through a circular economy, can help cities protect their water resources and address wastewater problems as they grow.

Oberbillwerder's Green Loop is part public realm, part climate adaptation. The open space allows residents and visitors to move about the district in natural areas without interacting with cars, and it doubles as temporary retention for stormwater events. (Credit: By ADEPT and Karres en Brands)

The circular economy can transform them in more sustainable and efficient ways, aided by designing out pollution and waste. This would reduce the amount of water waste, avoid pollution altogether or recover more water from pollution sources, protect clean water, and provide better capture and storage of water. Speaking of waste, although most ecodistricts do not go to this length, a handful of projects and districts have started looking at large-scale composting and wastewater management. The Living Building Challenge–certified Bullitt Center in Seattle was probably the most notable installation of composting toilets in the United States, but they were removed after seven years because of design problems and maintenance costs.[14] One of the main benefits of composting toilets is that they dramatically reduce water usage; the Bullitt Center used nearly 95 percent less water than an average commercial building. Composting toilets allow the possibility of recycling urine and feces into fertilizer. They also reduce the burden on urban wastewater systems.

Vienna's Seestadt (Lake City) features a large publicly accessible lake as recreational space and stormwater mitigation. (Credit: Lukasz Karnas)

The Swiss Coopérative d'Habitation Equilibre has installed several composting toilets in urban settings in some of their projects around Geneva. The cooperative has over ten years of experience with composting toilets in innovative multifamily projects. The thinner floor plates that on one hand allow more space for courtyards and urban heat island mitigation also allow more space for dealing with composting on site. The consultant on those projects, AnEco, is an organization that looks for sustainable and ecological sanitation solutions in urban areas.[15]

The feasibility of urine harvesting and humanure composting for urban agriculture was not on my radar a decade ago, but I find myself thinking about it way too much these days, and the climate implications cross in interesting ways. Just think about how many agricultural fossil fuels could be reduced by substituting urea from humans, as opposed to synthetic urea derived from fossil fuels.

Nature-based solutions and blue-green infrastructure will play an increasingly vital role in the livability and adaptability of urban areas. Developing more sustainable, adaptive, and inclusive cities is no longer an option for high-quality living. Rethinking urban loops, especially with regard to water and waste, may allow for creative solutions that position ecodistricts and cities that prioritize them to better adapt to the changes that will result from global warming.

CHAPTER 16

Active Resilience with Passive House

You wouldn't know it by looking at it, but the thermos or vacuum flask is one of the most ingenious inventions, a device that uses a vacuum to keep hot liquids hot, or cold liquids cold, for extended periods of time. It also happens to be one of the impetuses for the Passive House standard. Officially, Passive House is an ultra-low-energy building efficiency standard that also touches on climate change, sustainability, construction quality, and comfort. It is the only building standard I have come across that actively works to mitigate the effects of climate change. It also has an incredible number of co-benefits that help it stand out above other standards.

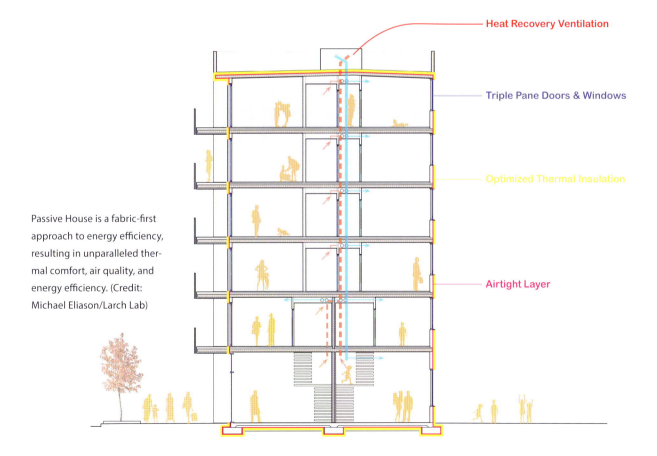

Passive House is a fabric-first approach to energy efficiency, resulting in unparalleled thermal comfort, air quality, and energy efficiency. (Credit: Michael Eliason/Larch Lab)

The Passive House standard was developed by European physicists Wolfgang Feist (Germany) and Bo Adamson (Sweden) in the late 1980s, with Feist founding the Passive House Institute (PHI) in Darmstadt in 1996. The Passive House standard is derived from research at the time on building science and energy conservation in Europe but influenced in large part by energy efficiency studies and experiments in the United States and Canada. One of those influential projects was the 1977 Saskatchewan Conservation House, by Harold Orr and William Shurcliff. The Saskatchewan House was one of the first to look at conservation, with every dollar spent on improving the thermal envelope to reduce heat loss having a tenfold effect on the use of solar equipment to achieve similar results. To do this, the house was designed to be airtight, with R-40 walls, an R-60 ceiling, triple-pane windows (at a time when even double pane was rare), and a heat recovery ventilator. Those principles form the foundation of the Passive House standard today.

The PHI is the main organization involved in research, planning, and design protocols for Passive House projects across a variety of building types, from detached houses to hospitals, and in all global climate zones. The first Passive House project was a four-unit rowhouse in Darmstadt-Kranichstein, Germany. It was built as a proof of concept, a research project, and notably a Baugruppe (see Chapter 11) where Feist's family came together with others to design and develop their homes.[1] In 2016, after residing in the development for twenty-five years, the PHI performed a study indicating that the building continues to perform incredibly well, even with components that would be considered less than high performance by today's standards. The study notes that the ventilation ducts were incredibly clean, after slight tuning the airtightness was nearly as good as when originally commissioned, the building envelope and windows continue to perform nearly as well as when brand new, and, most importantly, the energy consumption remains as low as modeled.[2]

What Is a Passive House, Exactly?

Passive House is a climate-specific building performance standard that has three requirements. First, the heating and cooling demand of a building space has to be less than 15 kilowatt-hours per square meter per year (or, in imperial terms, 4.75 kilo–British thermal units per square foot per year). This means that the maximum heating demand for a dwelling with a net internal reference area of 100 square meters (1,076 square feet) would be 1,500 kilowatt-hours per year. If energy costs are $0.10 per kilowatt-hour, then annual heating costs would be $150, less than the increase in average annual US heating bills[3] from 2021 to 2022. On top of the radical reductions

Airtightness is achieved through the use of gaskets, tapes, and membranes to ensure a continuous air barrier. (Credit: 475 High Performance Building Supply)

in energy consumption and operational carbon emissions, Passive House is also an effective approach to tackling energy poverty. Although historically the cost to build a Passive House has required a small increase in construction cost due to better-performing products and higher construction quality, the increase is nominal today as energy codes require higher levels of performance and efficiency. A recent Passive House Network report revealed that construction costs to achieve Passive House are getting closer to zero,[4] and even affordable housing projects meeting the Passive House standard are coming in on time and under budgeted construction costs.[5] As the Inflation Reduction Act ramps up, the cost benefits and parity of Passive House buildings will increase further.

Second, the project-specific primary demand, the overall energy consumption of the building, must be limited to 120 kilowatt-hours per square meter per year (or 38 kilo–British thermal units per square foot per year) for "classic" Passive House certification. This metric is the annual energy consumed on site (heating, hot water, lighting, and plug loads) multiplied by the grid emissions factor, a number reflecting the carbon emissions generated in the production of the local energy grid. In order to meet requirements for Passive House certification in regions with grids that have a high carbon mix, projects must be even more energy efficient. The good news is that the electrical grid is getting cleaner over time, thanks to renewables and the phase-out of carbon-intensive generation. The PHI has updated its own standard over time to reflect this improvement, offering certification classes (Plus, Premium) for even more energy efficiency and the production of on-site renewables. This is the preeminent path toward energy-positive buildings, or buildings that produce more energy than they consume. Because of their comprehensive nature and systematic approach to planning, Passive House buildings tend to use about half the energy of the most stringent energy codes enforced in the United States today. This leads to lower operational costs and significant reductions in the amount of carbon emitted in the operations of the building.

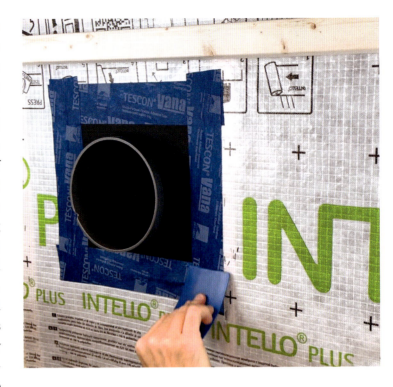

The third requirement is for an extreme level of airtightness, where the building has to pass a blower door test (a pressurization test) of 0.6 air changes per hour at 50 pascals. Airtightness is critical for drastically reducing heat loss and the movement of water vapor through the building. Air leakage in buildings is a bad thing. The Department of Energy has calculated that 25 to 40 percent of energy used for heating and cooling is due to air leakage.[6] Eliminating this source provides a number of benefits, including allowing for smaller mechanical systems, lowering energy bills, reducing drafts, improving comfort, reducing mold risk from condensation and vapor transfer, and improving air quality. The airtightness test is also a quality check: Buildings that are not constructed diligently and properly are unlikely to get anywhere close to this requirement.

The PHI has a number of recommendations to facilitate meeting these requirements. These include an optimized building envelope for opaque and transparent assemblies, airtightness, continuous ventilation, and thermal bridge–free construction. A thermal bridge is an area of a building where heat loss is increased by components in the construction, such as steel or

Gaskets and tape help keep out cold drafts, moisture, and wildfire smoke. (Credit: 475 High Performance Building Supply)

Continuous, fresh ventilation in Passive House buildings is supplied by heat recovery ventilators or energy recovery ventilators. High-efficiency filters prevent nearly all air pollution, dust, pollen, and wildfire smoke from entering the building. This photo shows clean and dirty filters for a home in Chicago, positioned a few blocks off a main arterial. (Credit: From Scott Farbman and Dr. Caroline Antler's home)

concrete members that have low thermal resistance and act like straws for heat flow. Passive House projects are modeled in the Passive House Planning Package, perhaps the most detailed Excel spreadsheet I've ever seen. The detailed model pays off, however, as the monitored results of the Passive House standard speak for themselves. Measured projects routinely perform as predicted, reducing energy costs significantly and avoiding sizable carbon emissions.

Optimized Building Envelopes

In order to minimize heat loss, the insulation of the solid portions of the building envelope must be continuous and optimized to prevent the flow of heat through exterior assemblies. This varies based on location: Colder climates will require higher R-values to minimize heat loss than warmer ones. There are also other factors at play: the internal heat loads of the building, occupant loads, and building form and compactness.

Transparent building components also need to have optimal R-values. Windows, doors, and skylights generally will need slightly higher-performing products than US energy codes require, but the good news is that for larger buildings, especially those planned as Passive House buildings from the beginning, these values aren't significantly higher. For most of the United States, triple-pane glazing will be needed. There are additional benefits to this as well, including a reduction in environmental noise, a noted benefit for those working or living on loud streets or airport approaches.

Airtightness

The airtightness requirement is achieved with a continuous air barrier that wraps completely around the building. This layer ensures that there is no air moving through the building's exterior assemblies, which drastically reduces cold drafts and the movement of water vapor and moisture through the assembly. This not only significantly reduces energy costs but also reduces mold risk in the building envelope. Several options are available to create this

Active Resilience with Passive House 137

continuous air barrier, including tapes, gaskets, membranes, liquid-applied and spray-applied products, sealants, and even gypsum. Every penetration of the building's envelope is critical in a Passive House, and the air barrier requires appropriate air sealing and attention in order to meet the pressurization standard, which is verified through a blower door test.

Continuous Fresh, Filtered Air

Since a Passive House is an airtight building, all rooms must be directly or indirectly supplied with fresh air. This is done primarily mechanically with a heat recovery ventilator or energy recovery ventilator. Think of this as the lungs of the building. The heat recovery ventilator continuously provides fresh air while extracting and exhausting stale air. The heat from the exhaust is captured and redirected to the incoming fresh air. These machines are incredibly efficient, quiet, and capable of recapturing up to 94 percent of the heat instead of wasting it by venting it outdoors. Energy recovery ventilators operate in a similar manner but are also able to recapture moisture in the exhaust air, to maintain a more stable relative humidity indoors. This process reduces the discomfort of incoming cold air, reduces mold risk, and reduces the amount of heating and cooling needed.

European tilt/turn windows allow fresh air in while providing security and protection from rain. They also allow solar shades on the exterior of the window or door to be raised or lowered without conflicts. In the United States, most windows swing or pivot outward, interfering with exterior solar protection. (Credit: Photo by Zola)

Wildfire Smoke–Resistant Buildings

Whether a building could be wildfire smoke resistant was not a question I ever anticipated having to field, and yet it is one I hear increasingly as a practicing architect. Historically, our buildings have been incredibly leaky and largely of poor construction. This has become problematic with the increasing prevalence of wildfire smoke events. This is where the synergies of Passive House shine. The airtight building envelope works almost flawlessly to keep out wildfire smoke and particulates. The continuous fresh air that

138 Building for People

is supplied to the building flows through filters (generally minimum efficiency reporting value 13) that filter out the majority of PM2.5 particulates, the fine, inhalable pollutants generated by wildfires that are dangerous to human health. There is even the possibility of adding a prefilter to the exterior at the ventilation system's intake, to further reduce the infiltration of particulates during smoke events.

In effect, the building acts as a system to protect the indoor air quality and the occupants. Those benefits are also applicable to people who live or work on or adjacent to highways, arterials, and railyards.[7] The fresh air, frequent air changes, and moderated internal temperatures and humidity can also reduce aerosol spread in future pandemics.

Public Health Wins, Too

There are so many co-benefits when it comes to Passive House, doctors should be prescribing it to patients at every opportunity. Schools end up with comfortable classrooms where carbon dioxide levels remain far lower than in typical construction,[8] ensuring a better learning environment for students. Passive House is great for employers, and before the COVID-induced work-from-home phenomenon, there were numerous reports of businesses seeing higher productivity and less absenteeism after they moved into a Passive House facility.[9] The incredibly low energy consumption of Passive House reduces energy poverty and protects against price spikes. The optimized thermal envelope and continuous fresh, filtered air ensure a level of indoor air quality that is almost unsurpassed. Residents in Passive House social housing in the United Kingdom have noted reduced severity of asthma, and mold growth is almost nonexistent in these projects.[10]

Climate Adaptation

What initially drew me to Passive House was how comfortable, efficient, and predictable it was compared with other building standards and the associated reduction in operational carbon emissions. The high quality of the interior environments and phenomenal air quality of a Passive House school I visited in Hanover, Germany, in 2011—far superior to that of any building I had ever been in—further cemented my opinion that this was the way buildings should be constructed. At Larch Lab, we try to ensure that all the buildings we design meet or exceed the Passive House standard. More recently, our focus has shifted to resilience, passive survivability, and climate adaptation,

Profile of Passive House triple-pane window providing superior acoustic and thermal performance over US code minimum windows. US energy codes won't require products this efficient until long after 2030. (Credit: Zola)

and these are all areas where Passive House is top in the field. When looking at the effects climate change will have on buildings—changes most planners have not really begun to even think about or react to—Passive House rises above other programs with a standard that functions well in today's conditions and promises to in future warming scenarios.

Heat due to climate change is a growing concern. The effects it will have on buildings are significant. In heat waves, a Passive House building will also be more resilient than code minimum construction. These are buildings that need minimal active cooling to remain habitable. Cooling loads can be shifted to off-peak times, reducing demand on the electrical grid.

During a power outage in cold weather, Passive House buildings stay warmer for significantly longer than typical construction. Occupants are protected from leaks inside the building due to pipes bursting in freezing temperatures. The Rocky Mountain Institute studied how long a home could remain habitable in an extended power outage during a cold snap and came up with an Hours-of-Safety measure. The study determined that a Passive House home can stay habitable longer,[11] with temperatures remaining above 40°F (152 hours) nearly twenty times as long as a home built in the 1950s (8 hours) and more than twice as long as a Net-Zero Energy Ready home (61 hours).

The level of protection against air pollution and wildfire smoke alone might be reason enough for most people to demand a Passive House. Other building standards may adapt to some of these types of events, but few can adapt as well as Passive House can.

The Passive House focus on minimizing heating and cooling gains and losses through the building envelope is also a means of futureproofing buildings. Because the loads are significantly smaller, the mechanical systems for these buildings end up being significantly smaller than what the energy codes require. There is an inherent beauty in this. In the future, when mechanical equipment reaches the end of its service life and needs to be replaced, the technology is likely to be even more effective. Not only are the first costs for mechanical equipment lower than typical construction, but the replacement costs decades later will also be lower.

Policy Levers

Currently, twenty-one cities opting in to the Massachusetts Stretch Code,[12] including Boston and Cambridge, are the only jurisdictions in the United States where Passive House levels of performance are mandated. Washington and

New York State have optional pathways for Passive House. The International Energy Conservation Code, the model ordinance that state energy codes are derived from, does not require performance levels anywhere close to Passive House. According to a recent study by Emu Building Science, even the 2024 International Energy Conservation Code energy code (which won't be in effect for most jurisdictions until after 2027 because of how energy codes are adopted) will perform well below the Passive House standard.[13] Cities and states have significant leverage in prioritizing climate adaptive building standards. Leadership in Energy and Environmental Design (LEED), a points-based green building standard developed by the US Green Building Council, has been the environmental standard for public works in the United States for several decades. Historically it has not been an indicator of radical reductions in energy consumption or building performance, and only recently has LEED certification required building performance metrics, with an option for just a 5 percent improvement over the worst-performing building possible.[14]

One approach cities and states could take would be to mandate the adoption of Passive House for new public buildings. Where state constitutions allow, a better approach is for cities to outright mandate Passive House levels of performance for all new buildings. This is effectively what Brussels did in 2011, to get ahead of the European Union's Energy Performance of Buildings Directive,[15] a policy that required new buildings meet high levels of energy performance starting in 2020. Brussels provided €45 million in economic incentives and promotion for developments that achieved Passive House.[16] There was an extensive Passive House training program for city staff, developers, tradespeople, and planners. The adoption of Passive House took off in Brussels, with the region becoming a lighthouse, and planners exporting their skills and knowledge to locations worldwide, including China, Africa, and New York City. The program in Brussels launched nearly 250 Passive House projects between 2007 and 2013, with hundreds more added since then across a variety of sizes, types, and scales—nearly a decade before the European Union's Nearly Zero Energy Building standard mandated similar levels of performance.

In 2023, Seattle citizens (including me) successfully lobbied for the passing of I-135, an initiative for a Social Housing Public Development Authority, tasked with building affordable housing built to the Passive House standard. It took little to convince the initiative's authors that the primary benefits and co-benefits of Passive House far exceeded those of any other standard. That numerous social housing providers in Europe, including Neue Heimat Tirol in Austria and ABG Frankfurt, are front runners in the adoption of Passive House for their affordable housing certainly helped.

Passive House is also a standard that pairs extremely well with other green building approaches, elevating the benefits of mass timber and decarbonized construction. Because of its focus on energy performance, many planning firms that are focused on Living Building Challenge certification, are already involved in Passive House. The two standards complement each other incredibly well, and a notable example is Hennebery Eddy's proposal for the Yellowstone Youth Campus in Mammoth, Wyoming, located in Yellowstone National Park.[17] These complementary effects have led to a cooperative agreement with the International Living Future Institute (the administering organization for the Living Building Challenge) and the PHI.[18]

In Heidelberg's mixed-use ecodistrict of Bahnstadt, a 1,400-home district built on a brownfield where Passive House was mandated, the monitored heating demand was in line with the standard at 15 kilowatt-hours per square meter per year, resulting in nearly 90 percent savings in total heating demand[19] (space heating, domestic hot water, distribution and storage losses) compared with other new, non–Passive House construction that was connected to the district heating system.

Passive House incentives and mandates could also boost innovation in manufacturing. China was a latecomer to the Passive House community but to date has 150 certified Passive House window frames.[20] Despite practitioners and developers beating China by nearly a decade, the United States only has thirty certified window profiles. Although there are a handful of ventilation manufacturers focused on Passive House in the United States, there is room for improvement for most of the major manufacturers, whose products do not come anywhere close to complying with the requirements for certification. Certainly, it seems that if we're going to "build back better," we should really aim to be building better in the first place. Passive House is the most direct and economical means of getting there.

CHAPTER 17

The Heat Is Already Here

Wildfire smoke has become an annual event in Seattle, and these events will continue to worsen as forests dry out. Although Passive House can mitigate most of the effects at the local level, there is no possibility to prevent climate-related wildfire events without dramatic reductions in greenhouse gases. (Credit: James Taylor)

In 2003 a heat wave in Europe claimed the lives of over 72,000 people.[1] I was in Germany at the time and have vivid memories of news reports showing rails and airport tarmacs buckling in the intense heat. This was the most oppressive weather I had ever experienced—that is, until the Pacific Northwest's 2021 heat dome that shattered hundreds of all-time record highs throughout Washington and Canada and reached an unbelievable 121°F in Lytton, British Columbia. Just two weeks prior, I was part of an American Institute of Architects Seattle panel on innovation and future-oriented housing. A noted developer stated that active cooling or air conditioning would not be needed in the Pacific Northwest in the future, because temperatures always

dropped down into the 50s at night. Just a few days later, the record temperatures and high humidity resulted in the deaths of 619 people in British Columbia[2] and of at least 441 people, directly or indirectly, in Washington State according to a University of Washington study.[3] Just two years later, extreme heat shattered annual heat records worldwide.[4]

The heat is not coming; it is already here.

Unfortunately, our politicians, buildings, and building industry are wholly unprepared for it.

Planning for the Heat

When I was a child, my father was in the Air Force, and we were fortunate enough to live in Germany and Belgium for almost a decade. This formative time introduced me to housing with features I had never seen before and have rarely seen since while living and working in the United States. One of the more intriguing features used almost universally on homes was some form of operable exterior shading. In Germany, a common option is roll-down external shutters called Rolladen. We used these at night, when it was hot out, for privacy, or even as additional security when leaving town. In my professional life, the only operable external shading in the United States has entailed either expensive custom fabricated solutions or solar protection products imported from Europe.

Exterior solar shading used to be fairly common in the United States. Awnings of all types and sizes were used on buildings until shortly after World War II, with the advent of air conditioning. The White House installed large awnings in the summer to keep out the heat.[5] During the Truman administration, an extensive renovation introduced air conditioning to the White House,[6] and the awnings were no longer needed to keep cool. I note this because it illustrates that we used to use passive strategies to keep places cool and habitable without consuming exorbitant quantities of energy, even in fairly tropical conditions.

With the advent of air conditioning and cheap energy, the US direction on buildings and climate was different from that of places like Europe, where energy has generally been more expensive. This peculiar difference even affects window types and how they are manufactured and operated. In Europe, with exterior shutters and roll-down blinds, windows generally open inward. This allows occupants to close the blinds partially or fully yet keep the windows and doors open to maximize the inflow of breezes. Windows in the United

A

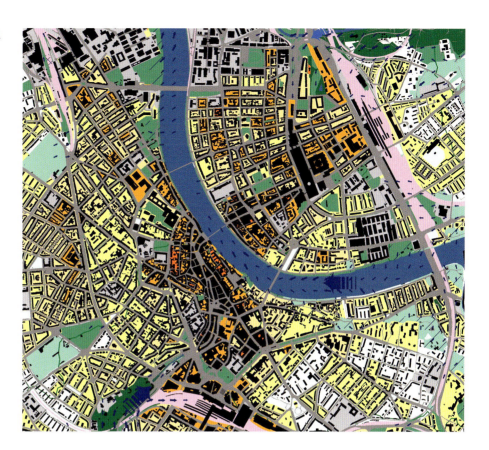

B

Cities leading on climate are modeling how increased temperatures will affect neighborhoods and residents. Basel, Switzerland, has started to incorporate future climate models into urban planning decisions, analyzing existing bioclimatic situations at the block level (A) compared with anticipated warming through 2030 (B). This can indicate which measures will work best in different locations. (Credit: Bau- und Verkehrsdepartment des Kantons Basel-Stadt)

States tend to open outward, with shades placed on the interior. This makes no sense from an energy standpoint because the most effective position to locate shading to reduce overheating and subsequent cooling loads is on the exterior side of the glazing, where shading can reduce up to 90 percent of solar gain on the interior.

The Risks of Overheating

Climate change is bringing about an increase in the frequency and duration of extreme heat events. This will be a significant liability in a warming world, especially in countries with no active solar protection industry. In 2021, law firm Berding & Weil announced a $10 million settlement they had procured between a developer and residents of a new condo building in San Francisco, a city famous for its incredibly mild climate. The release stated, "We further demonstrated that on sunny days when the outdoor temperature was mild the units could get as hot as 90 degrees without the ability to cool off, making the interior environment of the units unbearable."[7]

With no external shading devices, and probably an inability to cross-ventilate, those south- and west-facing dwellings became unbearable in mild weather. Our building codes do not result in multifamily housing that can cross-ventilate, and our energy codes do not mandate exterior solar protection or even active cooling. As temperatures rise and heat-related power outages become more common,[8] these buildings can become deadly.[9]

The British Columbia coroner's report stated that many of the deaths from the Pacific Northwest heat dome were older adults, overheating in small homes without cooling and, perhaps more importantly, without a social network that was able to check on residents. I assume that the majority of these homes were in double-loaded corridors and lacked the ability to cross-ventilate. Older adults are especially vulnerable to the effects of extreme heat.[10]

Many European cities have begun to look at the effects of future warming scenarios in their urban planning and at how warm districts or neighborhoods, including Freiburg and Basel, will be between 2070 and 2100 under various warming scenarios. Basel's Urban Climate Concept[11] even looks at how various settlement types (perimeter blocks, slab buildings, villas) are anticipated to perform during heat events. Monitoring, measuring, and mitigation are what cities and planners should be thinking about to ensure that buildings and neighborhoods will remain habitable during extreme temperature events.

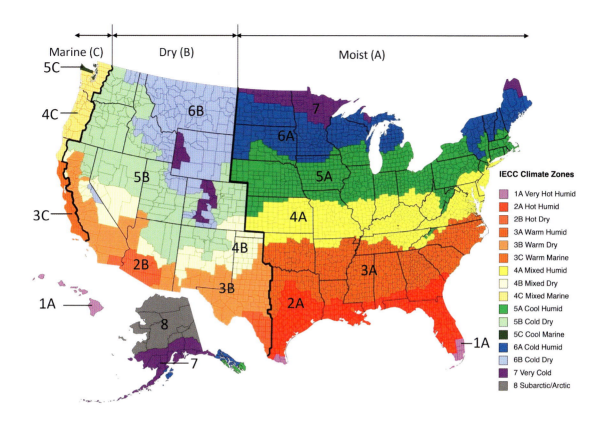

Climate Zone Migration

Our buildings were designed for a climate that no longer exists.

The energy models for Passive House projects are highly tuned to the climate in which they are built. However, climate data are based on historic averages. The Passive House Institute has developed a tool that allows planners to see how buildings will perform in warming scenarios. The tool is very easy to use, and it can be quite eye opening to see a building that is tuned to perform exceedingly well in its climate zone but is projected to perform quite poorly as climate zones migrate.

There are eight climate zones in the United States, developed through research from the Pacific Northwest National Lab for the Department of Energy (DOE).[12] The zones range from hot to subarctic, with further subdivisions on moisture—humid (A), dry (B), and marine (C)—for a total of twenty-four possible zones. If you follow climate discussions or are an avid gardener, these maps are somewhat similar to Köppen–Geiger Climate Map classifications. The DOE's climate zone map is used by the nonprofit International Code Council for developing the International Energy Conservation Codes (the part of the building code related to thermal envelope performance and energy consumption). The American Society of Heating, Refrigerating and

The United States is broken up into different climate zones, based on regional historic data. With climate change, climate zones are going to migrate north, causing severe problems with building envelopes built for colder climates. (Credit: IECC 2021)

The Heat Is Already Here 147

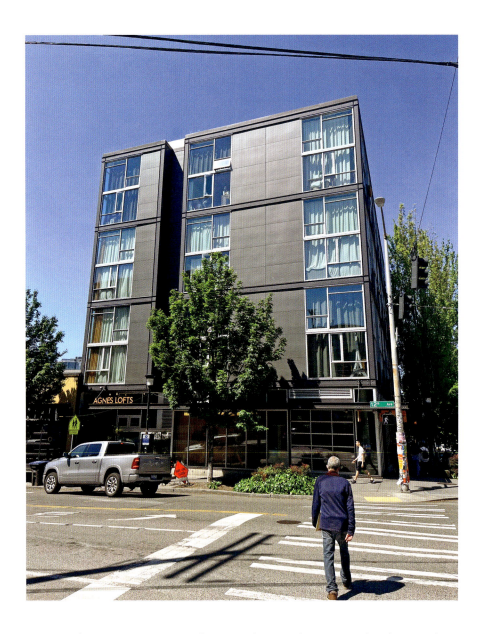

Air-Conditioning Engineers also uses the DOE's maps in developing their standards for buildings.

Here is the problem: Historic local climate data are used for the design conditions in energy modeling and predicted energy performance of buildings. These are the metrics used for designing the walls and roofs to reduce energy loss and for sizing mechanical equipment. The effects of climate change are going to radically alter the way buildings perform: Places that were cold will become warm or even hot, places that were dry will become wet, and places that have never needed active cooling will need to provide it. As the average temperatures increase with climate change, the peak highs and lows will become more extreme. These effects have already been seen in recent years,

The lack of active solar protection in new construction will increasingly become a liability for developers and architects, even in mild climates like Seattle's. This problem is exacerbated by double-loaded corridor buildings where occupants can't cross-ventilate or night purge. (Credit: Michael Eliason)

with the Pacific Northwest's 2021 heat dome and the Great Texas Freeze that same year. These extreme billion-dollar weather events led to severe discomfort and death, broken pipes and associated flooding, illness, heat stroke, and homes that became temporarily uninhabitable or even deadly. These extremes, as well as future climate impacts, will need to be considered in the planning of buildings and districts.

A 2015 National Aeronautics and Space Administration study looked at how climate zones will migrate under high and baseline emissions.[13] Imagine Atlanta's Climate Zone 3A (warm, humid) migrating up to Minneapolis, whose Climate Zone 6A (cold, humid) is known for extremely cold and hardy winters. Well, it may not be something to imagine, as the study showed that under a high-emissions scenario (RCP8.5), this is a possibility between 2071 and 2100 in the warmest models. From a building science perspective, this is problematic. The way that walls and roofs are designed in a heating-dominated climate in order to keep out the cold and the layers of materials used within walls to reduce air and moisture movement are incredibly different from how walls are designed in a cooling-dominated climate. Not only will increasing temperatures increase the risk of overheating in buildings designed to a previous climate, but climate zone migration will increase the risk of moisture problems and potential mold growth in wall and roof assemblies. There is also an increased risk of mold associated with climate change and increased frequencies of precipitation.[14]

The Question of Air Conditioning

Like that developer on the American Institute of Architects Seattle panel, I used to believe that living without air conditioning in mild climates like the Pacific Northwest would be possible, even with global warming. I no longer believe that. Unfortunately, reliance on air conditioning makes matters worse. The subject is intermingled with numerous problems, including increased peak energy loads that can lead to brownouts, inequitable access to cooling,[15] increasing temperatures from equipment,[16] and refrigerants that exacerbate global warming. There have been improvements in the fluorinated refrigerants in heat pumps, but the leakage rate of these refrigerants is high, which can increase greenhouse gas emissions, and so robust refrigerant management programs are needed.[17]

Low-income residents and renters face larger hurdles in accessing cooling, especially in places that have not historically needed them. Outside the United States, where inequality is even higher, the inequitable access to cooling is even more pronounced.

Designing Out the Heat

During the Pacific Northwest's 2021 heat dome, in our own home, with adequate solar shading and the ability to cross-ventilate, internal low temperatures remained above 85°F. It was unbearable, and we eventually decamped for family nearby who had air conditioning. We have friends and acquaintances who live in west-facing dwellings in new double-loaded corridor buildings who reported that the internal temperature in their dwelling never dropped below 90°F, even as exterior temps dropped into the 60s at night.

A common complaint about new construction in the United States is that building façades are incredibly flat, a problem that has even been written about in the *New York Times*.[18] There are several reasons for this flatness, including weak energy codes and thinner wall assemblies than in many other countries. Our façades also don't typically need to account for thick external insulation and shading devices, as are typically the case in European construction. This generally positions the glass of windows on US buildings close to the face of the exterior finish material, leaving small window reveals with little depth between the exterior face of window and façade and little opportunity for even modest relief from the sun. This also leaves windows more exposed to the elements.

If you look at new construction in much of Europe, the windows tend to have fairly significant reveals. This provides a number of surprising benefits, including better protection from the elements and better solar protection. The wall assemblies are generally thicker because of construction types generally using solid construction such as mass timber, clay block, or concrete, with rigid insulation added to the exterior of the wall. Windows tend to be placed in the middle of the wall assembly (which is fairly optimal from an energy efficiency standpoint). This positioning allows the housing for the exterior solar protection to be fastened directly to the structure, in line with the external insulation layer.

This subtle difference in wall thickness and insulation location on the exterior of the wall structure is critical for accommodating external shading devices. As an added benefit, deeper window reveals result in buildings that tend to look better, adding relief and variation to the façade that is absent in most US construction.

When I was working in Bayern, I was floored by the various active solar protection products at my disposal. What follows is a small sampling of those choices.

Roll-Down Shades

Operable external solar protection, such as roll-down shades, shutters, and awnings, is common in much of Europe. It is the most effective way to reduce overheating and associated cooling loads. There are almost no external shading manufacturers in the United States. (Credit: Michael Eliason)

Rolladen, or roll-down shades, are a shading product with connected horizontal blades, typically aluminum, that can be rolled up into a housing when not needed.

They feature a wide variety of finishes, with numerous color and material options available. The blades can come as solid elements or can feature microperforations or even custom patterns to block most of the sunlight. Historically, these have been hand operated, with a crank or a pulley integrated into the wall. However, in the last decade numerous electrified options that are operated by switch or remote have been introduced to the market. These can be integrated with building management systems to optimize cooling needs at the building scale. Although this is better from a thermal standpoint, because there are fewer penetrations or thermal bridges in the wall, there are limitations in heat-induced power outages. A handful of skylight (Dachfenster) manufacturers in Europe offer exterior roll-down shades that provide solar protection, hail protection, and privacy. The west-facing skylights in our apartment in Bayern had them, and they were great at keeping cool interior temperatures even on extremely hot days.

External Venetian Blinds

External venetian blinds are a solar protection product featuring horizontal slats, offering a significant amount of control for users. In the United States, venetian blinds can be found on the interior side of windows, largely for privacy and slight solar protection. The external variation typically features vertical cords or cables that the slats are affixed to. These slats can rotate from nearly vertical, offering the most solar protection and privacy; to horizontal, allowing for views and airflow, with a large amount of protection from direct sun; or to something in between, allowing for greater control or fine tuning. Like roll-down shades, these also come in a variety of colors and materials. The horizontal slats can be solid or perforated. Increasingly, these are also electronically controlled, connected to a building management system. External venetian blinds were used to reduce the cooling demand for Seattle's Bullitt Center by Miller Hull, the most energy-efficient commercial building in the United States at the time it was built in 2013. Unsurprisingly, these blinds were manufactured by Warema, a German company.

Drop Arm Awnings

Drop arm awnings feature a retractable awning and an arm that drops as the awning is unfolded, projecting the awning outward from the face of the wall. This provides better protection from the sun while still allowing views in or out. This arrangement also allows for more use of breezes than other systems and can help keep out rain while windows are open. These are fairly common on homes, schools, and shops in Mediterranean environments. The projected awning can break up the façade or add a splash of color. A variation includes a guiding tube that keeps a portion of the awning parallel to the façade; then it drops diagonally to the projecting arm. The awning material is typically a fabric such as acrylic or polyester. They are offered in numerous colors or translucencies.

Operable Shutters

Operable exterior shutters come in a variety of types, including folding and sliding. They can be solid, louvered, or perforated. Options for wood or metal abound; there is almost an unlimited amount of creativity possible with them. They can add detail and relief to the façade. These are also some of my favorite approaches because they are generally manual and thus can remain functional during power outages if they are accessible. These are much more common in Europe, on every type of housing including social housing.

Sail Shades

These shades tend to be shaped like a sail and are installed in tension. They are typically found along exterior spaces, such as balconies or loggia, roof decks, or terraces. Sail shades incorporate anchors that attach to the sail. They tend to be significantly less expensive than retractable awnings and are generally manually installed and demounted. Some models are retractable; these can be found in larger public spaces. When I was working in Germany, these were incorporated into nearly every school or kindergarten project the office worked on. Architect and Passive House designer Juraj Mikurcik used sail shades on his own prefabricated straw panel house, in order to prevent solar gain from overheating the interior and keep his patio comfortable. Sail shades are a low-tech, low-cost solution with high benefit.

Trees and Greenery

Trees are a great way to provide exterior shade and mitigate the urban heat island effect[19] at both the building and district scale. The use of a trellis with

Sail shades can also be effective solar protection and can be found on roof decks, playgrounds, and even homes, as in this self-build straw panel Passive House in Herefordshire, England. (Credit: Juraj Mikurcik)

greenery is another option that used to be popular on housing and is making a comeback as cities try to induce more green façades, although there are height limitations. Some of the more intriguing examples I've seen include espaliers, hops, and even vineyards as a more productive option for seasonal exterior shading. Cologne even has a city vintner who can help groups determine the best types of grapes to grow on their buildings or in their yards. One of our neighbors in Bayern had grapevines growing over his south-facing terrace and windows, and it smelled amazing during the fall harvest.

Designing Out the Heat

There are three steps that politicians, designers, and planners should be prioritizing to design out the heat. The first is to prevent overheating due to solar gain entering the building in the first place, either with fixed shades, or ideally, operable exterior shading. A 2022 study modeling the passive survivability of multifamily housing during heat events in the Pacific Northwest noted that without shading and natural ventilation, "dangerous heat indices occurred frequently even before the heat wave occurred, illustrating the vulnerability to extreme heat that exists when shading and operable windows are unavailable."[20] This study also showed that exterior shading alone produced a 40 percent reduction in cooling load and, when combined with fan-assisted ventilation, an 80 percent reduction.

The second step is to prioritize designs that are able to incorporate natural ventilation and cross-ventilation, specifically with point access blocks,

single-loaded corridors, and similar access strategies discussed in chapter 6. Urban form can also play a role, allowing or restricting the movement of air. This is a giant leap from a status quo where double-loaded corridors are the norm. However, in a world that is likely to see significantly warmer temperatures and increasing power outages, that ability to adapt will be crucial.

The third step is that cooling will be needed in most areas, but our energy codes should be planned so that the cooling loads are as small as possible, with incentives to use the most decarbonized cooling system possible. This is one of the things that attracted me to Passive House, because it is so energy efficient that the amount of energy needed to heat or cool is incredibly low. Using only what is needed is preferable to having poorly performing buildings

There are a number of co-benefits with climate adaptation. Trees can help mitigate the urban heat island effect, provide space for biodiversity, and create enjoyable places for people to gather. (Credit: Michael Eliason)

154 Building for People

where we use an absurd amount of energy to cool them. At the district scale, economies of scale can be applied for determining lower-carbon methods of cooling buildings.

Overheating will increasingly become a liability for builders, architects, and planners,[21] who have a duty of care to ensure that their buildings do not become dangerous or uninhabitable with the known effects of climate change. It remains to be seen whether politicians, planners, or developers will act. My hope is that building and energy codes transition to account for these conditions in the next few years so that architects and builders can incorporate locally manufactured solutions to ensure that homes remain survivable and adaptable to new extremes.

PART IV

Building Decarbonization

158 Building for People

CHAPTER 18

Circular Mass Timber Districts

"Reforest the planet, retimber the city: We need to create an alternative carbon sink in the built environment and wood construction is the perfect answer."

—John Schellnhuber, Intergovernmental Panel on Climate Change author and founding director of the Potsdam Institute for Climate Impact Research

Top, Dowel laminated timber is a stunning, all-wood prefabricated mass timber component that I have been trying to incorporate into projects since first working with it in Freiburg in 2003–2004. (Credit: Michael Eliason)

Left, Mass timber components such as DLT, CLT, and glulam columns and beams can be erected quickly, with fewer deliveries than concrete or steel and lower carbon footprints because of their lightweight character. Pictured is LEVER Architecture's Albina Yard in Portland during construction. (Credit: LEVER Architecture)

The construction industry is heavily resource extractive and produces significant quantities of waste. Many of the processes and materials can be quite toxic, and most materials are not reusable. High-value products are downcycled, losing their value. The way we are building and developing cities needs a drastic transformation, and a circular built environment may be the best approach to counteract a wasteful status quo. Through the sufficiency principle, resources can be conserved and deployed in a smarter and more efficient manner. Transitioning to a circular economy and using circular construction will have massive positive economic effects, and positive environmental effects, reducing resource extraction and waste and conserving large amounts of embodied carbon.

My family's move to Bayern in 2019 was an attempt to situate myself in the heart of Europe's mass timber industry, where circularity, prefabrication, and innovation abound. Before we moved, I was the project manager for a small office project incorporating one of the first installations of dowel laminated timber (DLT) in the United States. DLT is a stunning panelized wood product made of lumber laid on end, with holes spaced regularly through the middle and a friction fit hardwood dowel connecting it all. No glues, no nails, and it looks beautiful. This project was poignant for me. When I was working in Freiburg years earlier, nearly every project incorporated DLT. I was *finally* working on the kind of project I had spent most of the previous decade striving for.

DLT is one of many products that make up a class of manufactured wood components called mass timber. Although building with large pieces of timber has been done for centuries and continues through today, *mass timber* is a term for construction using prefabricated, solid, or engineered wood elements to erect buildings that are lighter, stronger, and more ecological than carbon-intensive steel or concrete. These elements include cross-laminated timber (CLT) panels, DLT, glue-laminated columns and beams, and other value-added wood products. The roots of mass timber are found in Germany,[1] Austria, and Switzerland. Thanks to knowledge sharing and demand for higher-quality buildings, a sizable movement is under way in North America. The Woodworks Innovation Network maintains a map of the hundreds of mass timber projects in the United States.[2]

Benefits of Mass Timber

There are a number of benefits and co-benefits to the use of mass timber. It is incredibly strong and lightweight. This lighter weight means that mass timber typically requires far fewer construction site deliveries than concrete.[3] Foundations can also be significantly smaller than those of concrete or steel buildings. At Murray Grove, a nine-story cross-laminated timber project in Hackney, London, designed by Waugh Thistleton and completed in 2009, mass timber allowed for a 70 percent reduction in foundations, lowering costs and embodied carbon.[4]

The thermal properties of mass timber are superior to those of concrete, masonry, and steel, making it easier to design and build low-energy and Passive House buildings. The prefabricated elements minimize site waste. Just-in-time delivery ensures that the products are delivered to the site when needed and erected immediately. The erection crew needed for a mass timber building is small, and the process is both safer and quieter than typical construction.

Because mass timber is lighter than concrete, it enables interesting and creative ways to reintensify existing buildings. One approach is the Aufstockung, or vertical addition, allowing new homes to be added on top of existing buildings with prefabricated, lightweight wood components or systems. Another approach is to reuse existing concrete foundations for new buildings, reducing the need for additional concrete and associated embodied carbon and construction costs.

On top of all of this, mass timber may offer significant environmental benefits. The embodied carbon of construction is lower than that of concrete

Munich's Prinz-Eugen-Park is an ecodistrict with a focus on incorporation of wood building components. Team^3 is a Passive House Baugruppe designed by ArchitekturWerkstatt Vallentin with Johannes Kaufmann Architektur. (Credit: Lukas Vallentin)

or steel, and it is often stated that 1 ton of mass timber sequesters 1 ton of carbon dioxide. The use of mass timber incorporating wood thinned from forests could be one approach to derisking wildfires.[5] However, whether the biogenic carbon stored in wood does sequester carbon is still a question to many. Issues of sourcing and long-term forest health need to be addressed. Most of these can be mitigated through chain-of-custody certification, better forest management, and transparency. The mass timber industry in North America has had some significant setbacks, with production facilities delayed and manufacturers going bankrupt[6] despite significant demand.

Mass Timber Districts

With solid wood elements functioning as columns, beams, walls, floors, and roof elements, mass timber pairs incredibly well with midrise urban development. The sufficiency principle should be kept in mind when working with mass timber. Although it may be appropriate for midrise applications, for most low-rise applications the volume of wood that would be used with a mass timber structure far exceeds what wood-framed construction would

require because of the laminations. In these instances, prioritizing wood-framed construction for low-rise and even midrise construction may be optimal to use resources across a broader number of projects while allowing for equivalent levels of performance.

The case for mass timber districts is already being made. In Berlin, the award-winning Quartier Wir by Deimel Oelschlaeger Architekten, a block-sized district with 114 homes for roughly 250 residents, features a broad unit mix, including family-sized and cluster apartments, spread across five buildings surrounding a pedestrianized courtyard. The small district includes community spaces, a small pool, a play area for children, a daycare, and a café,[7] with the amenities arranged on the ground floor to activate the courtyard. The buildings are also designed to meet the Passive House standard. According to the architects, 6,000 cubic meters of wood used in the project takes about three hours to grow in German forests.[8]

In Munich, Prinz-Eugen-Park features nearly 1,800 homes, a third of which are a separate model ecodistrict featuring mass timber or wood hybrid buildings. The district features a school, several daycare facilities, a community center, a swimming pool, and a pedestrianized plaza with commercial spaces,

Prinz-Eugen-Park looking across the garden houses and point access block toward adjacent areas of the district. (Credit: Lukas Vallentin)

162 Building for People

View across the gardens and natural play area, toward the project. Aiming for Passive House ensures a high level of comfort, and building with mass timber keeps the carbon footprint of the project low. (Credit: Lukas Vallentin)

affordable co-working spaces, a grocery store, and a café. The tram-adjacent district features a number of different green and open spaces, the intention being different types for all.[9] The model ecodistrict is 50 percent affordable housing, with nonmarket cooperatives and Baugruppen providing another 25 percent. Several buildings also meet Passive House, including the team3 project, a Baugruppe developed by several nonprofits and designed by ArchitekturWerkstatt Vallentin with Johannes Kaufmann. The project is thirty-six homes in a variety of building types: garden houses, atrium houses, and flats in point access blocks.[10]

Berlin may see the largest mass timber district in the world. The Schumacher Quarter at Tegel will feature 5,000 homes, with the aim of wood being incorporated into at least 50 percent of buildings. The development team is calling it Bauhuette 4.0, a nod to the history of the trade associations that built social housing in Berlin and Industry 4.0 technologies possible with the value-added wood industry. The development is currently in planning, and the first buildings are projected to be completed in 2027, with the development fully built out by 2035. It includes a number of ambitious goals, including carbon storage and promotion of climate neutrality, transformation of the European building culture toward a bio-based circular economy, finding cost-effectiveness with scalable innovative production processes, multistory wood buildings in cities, digitizing production, and strengthening Industry 4.0.[11]

A 2022 study led by researchers at the Potsdam Institute for Climate Impact Research found that "if ninety percent of the new urban population would be housed in newly built urban mid-rise buildings with wooden constructions, 106 Gt of additional CO_2 could be saved by 2100."[12] Importantly, the study noted that the timber plantations needed for these four- to twelve-story midrise buildings could be grown without competing with agricultural production. Reductions in land use due to changes in diet, especially lands associated with dairy and meat production, are one such possibility and are already associated with reduced emissions.[13]

Mass Timber 2.0

Although mass timber has enjoyed a moment in the last few years, there is abundant room for improvement and innovation. Numerous products are being developed that will enable more resilient wood buildings. The US Forest Service's Wood Innovations program awards grants for the development and deployment of wood-based products and buildings.[14] The New European Bauhaus is all in on circular construction and decarbonized buildings, and prefabricated wood accounts for nearly 20 percent of all multifamily housing in Sweden[15] and 6 percent and growing in Germany.[16] The value-added wood industry in Europe has been running circles around the US industry.

The path to maximizing decarbonization in mass timber and the construction industry goes through circular construction. What happens to the wood panels at the end of the building's lifespan has a significant effect on lifecycle carbon emissions. If the panels are just landfilled, then the methane decays into the atmosphere. The wood could be burned for energy, which is better than landfilling. However, the path that offers the most reduction in carbon is reusing the components to extend their lifecycle.

Circular Construction

Circular construction requires considerable collaboration, transparency, and knowledge sharing, and additional labor and effort may be necessary in the planning phases.[17] It includes strategies such as design for disassembly, reusing, repurposing, refurbishing, remanufacturing, and upcycling. Resource-efficient design, optimization, reversible connections, prefabrication, and flexibility are critical components of circular construction.

Design for disassembly allows the elements to be taken apart at the end of the building's lifespan and used elsewhere rather than landfilled. It is a form of both resource and value capture, generally using distinct elements and mechanical fastening as opposed to casting, welding, or adhering building components together. Design for disassembly is driven by component-based and system-based approaches, where elements can be easily erected and demounted. In 2017, as Vienna's Parliament was undergoing renovations, three temporary buildings sprang up in just six months to house the staff and functions. The buildings were constructed of a demountable wood component-based system designed and fabricated by Lukas Lang Building Technologies. When the renovation was finished three years later, the buildings were dismantled and returned to the fabricator for deployment on other projects.[18] The system is incredibly smart and compact, and it allows components to be reused over and over again as needed, with minimal shipping.

One of the tools recognized as being necessary to shift to a circular built environment is the material passport, a digital set "of data describing defined characteristics of materials and components in products and systems that give them value for present use, recovery, and reuse."[19] The data for these passports are being developed and refined on circular projects in development. Buildings in a circular economy become material banks, and material passports list the ingredients that make up a building, highlighting what went into the building, where it is located, where it came from, and so forth. These data are necessary so that future users can assess what is in their buildings and what sort of material stocks they have access to and could also be used in lifecycle assessments or potential building certification programs.

There are numerous advantages to use of mass timber over typical construction, from aesthetics to construction speed to carbon reductions. Circular mass timber is ideal for midrise development. Circular concepts ensure that the lifespan of these durable, low-carbon components is significantly longer through reuse. Cities and developers should be looking to lead with these high-quality, comfortable, and low-carbon homes, schools, and offices in dense ecodistricts.

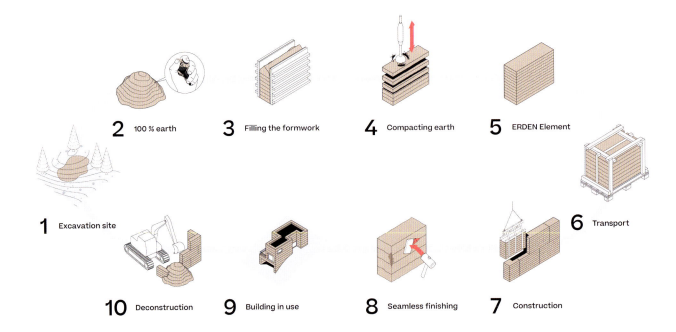

CHAPTER 19

Decarbonized Buildings

"My vision is entire cities of earth and multi-storey residential buildings that provide a wonderful indoor climate with a small ecological footprint. There's enough material to do so, and it would also be a fascinating story with respect to form."

—Martin Rauch, principal and founder of Lehm Ton Erde

The built environment is responsible for a significant amount of direct and indirect carbon emissions, accounting for nearly 40 percent of carbon emissions emitted annually.[1] A low-tech building product (such as a 2×4) can be matched with high-tech processes to transform it into a large-format element that can be used for multiple purposes and have multiple benefits. Pairing industrialized processes with low-tech products allows for some rather incredible building solutions that can be very low carbon, or even carbon neutral as industrial processes decarbonize. The options available to architects and engineers today, and the data to ensure their performance, are so much greater than even a decade ago. It's an incredible feat of human ingenuity that it is possible to build an entire district almost entirely without fossil fuel–derived building materials and concrete. It turns out nature-based solutions are great not only for carbon sequestration and climate adaptation but also for planning decarbonized buildings.

A building lifecycle assessment (LCA) is the total accounting of emissions, specifically greenhouse gases, released over its lifespan. This includes emissions from extraction and manufacturing of building products, erection, the operational usage of the building, repairs and rehabilitations, and material end-of-life decisions. LCAs can be used for a number of reasons, including studying impacts of design variations, declaring a building's performance, and documenting performance for ecological purposes.[2] It is a process that requires planners to really think about the total footprint of their building,

Lehm Ton Erde has figured out a process for building prefabricated rammed earth elements in a climate-controlled factory, which are delivered and installed on site. The process is completely circular, as cement binder is avoided, allowing the wall to be returned to nature at the end of life. (Credit: Sami Akkach, Lehm Ton Erde)

and it is increasingly becoming mandatory for planning permission. In 2023, California governor Gavin Newsom signed a bill requiring LCAs for buildings larger than five homes or 10,000 square feet, to be implemented by 2029.[3] Denmark now requires all buildings greater than 1,000 square meters (10,760 square feet) to submit LCAs, with a maximum limit of 2.5 pounds of carbon dioxide per square foot per year over a fifty-year period.[4] This is intended to ensure that new construction is actually sustainable and meets Denmark's climate goals.

First, Do No Harm

The embodied carbon footprint of new buildings typically is significantly higher than that of renovations, and so the first rule for building decarbonization is to reuse existing buildings. An open letter from German architects to Klara Geywitz, Germany's federal minister for housing, urban development, and construction, stated that over half of the waste generated in Germany comes from the construction industry, and it called for "preservation, renovation, conversion and further construction of the existing building, instead of demolitions for new buildings."[5] Taking account of existing building stocks and their associated components can allow diverting, repairing, and reusing building products to avoid waste streams.

Many ecodistricts opt to preserve and reuse existing structures for a variety of purposes: markets, workshops, community spaces, and institutions. Several others still will deconstruct existing buildings, with the salvaged components being repurposed in other buildings or landscapes. One of the more intriguing reuses I've seen proposed is the competition won by ASTOC with Bauchplan for the largely vacant Blautal-Center mall in Ulm, which will be converted into a mixed-use ecodistrict. New buildings will use existing foundations (a really great use case for lightweight mass timber elements), prefabricated stairs will be reincorporated into new buildings, and the underground parking will be reused. The site will feature a car-free center and 1,000 homes.[6]

Planning districts and buildings to have an extended lifespan is also a smart approach to decarbonization. Ensuring that a building is flexible beyond a generation or two, especially in the face of dramatic demographic shifts, is also important. As with housing, the secondary effect of incredibly deep floor plates in office buildings is a reduction in flexibility and adaptation to other uses; this problem is less common in countries that have daylighting requirements or regulations on floor plate depth. One of the largest effects

Rammed earth is a construction method that has a unique and awe-inspiring character. It also has a fairly low carbon footprint if cement is not used as a binder. It can also be used for floors. (Credit: Michael Eliason)

became obvious during the pandemic with the increase in work from home. As commercial building values crash due to significantly increased vacancy rates—a McKinsey study projected up to $800 billion in losses in just nine "superstar" cities through 2030[7]—the deep floor plates will make it incredibly difficult to convert to housing or other uses. Some of this problem could have been avoided if policies had been in place to require thinner buildings that would have been easier to convert to other uses.

Decarbonizing Structures

In college, I took a design–build studio course that designed and built a rammed earth farmhouse. The process was straightforward but incredibly time and labor intensive. It isn't really scalable, which makes multistory projects difficult. However, there have been phenomenal advances in the last two decades. In Austria, rammed earth pioneer Martin Rauch runs Erden, a company that can prefabricate rammed earth components and walls up to 12 feet long and 4 feet high off-site in a climate-controlled workshop.[8] The process has become increasingly industrialized, and exterior walls can even incorporate foamed glass gravel as insulation, which is necessary for comfort because the thermal properties of rammed earth are only slightly better than those of concrete. It's also a circular construction method, as walls can be deconstructed and returned to the earth. The versatility of prefabricated rammed earth is quite high, and it is not limited to low-rise buildings. In Heilbronn, Erden is collaborating with haas cook zemmrich STUDIO2050 for six-story midrise housing with rammed earth and mass timber.[9] For someone who spent weeks of his life at age twenty-two inside formwork, tamping down layers of earth to build a wall, seeing the advances the industry has made is jaw-dropping.

Structural stone is also making a comeback because of its low-carbon properties. In the United Kingdom, architecture firm Groupwork, led by Amin Taha, has done extensive work and research with structural engineering firm Webb Yates about the carbon reduction capabilities of stone for structural elements, as well as cut bricks. This includes impressive pre- and post-tensioned long-span beams capable of reaching lengths of 50 feet. Research for a thirty-story tower led by Groupwork revealed superior fire resistance and potential for cost savings of up to 75 percent, with up to 95 percent less embodied carbon emitted compared with a concrete and steel tower.[10] A French study noted that potential carbon reductions using cut stone in multifamily housing were significant over low-carbon concrete incorporating slag or even cross-laminated timber.[11] Not only is the carbon footprint of stone significantly lower than that of concrete, but it is durable and reusable. What is old is new again, and another fine candidate for decarbonized midrise buildings.

Eight percent of annual global carbon emissions are due to the production of concrete,[12] and the process is incredibly extractive. Although lower-carbon concrete has been feasible for years, negative- or zero-carbon concrete is slowly becoming a possibility and is necessary for meeting our climate goals. However, it is my belief that we should be aiming to use as little concrete as possible—in our buildings, in our districts, and in our rights of way.

Low-Carbon Finishes

Repair and replacement of elements and systems over time can contribute greatly to the total embodied carbon footprint of a building. Low-carbon interior finishes are critical not just for decarbonization but for ensuring high-quality interior environments with low levels of volatile organic compounds. Magnesium oxide board is a low-carbon replacement for gypsum board, used to finish interior walls. Pigmented clay plaster finishes are a durable and stunning low-carbon replacement for acrylic paints derived from fossil fuels. Clay plaster regulates interior humidity levels and can be applied directly to prefabricated exterior straw panels. Earthen floors are a nearly carbon-free substitute for concrete or gypsum concrete floors, can incorporate in-floor radiant heating, and are fully recyclable. Today, the reliance on vinyl and other fossil fuel–derived building products in typical construction is rampant. Planning teams should be incorporating durable and circular low-carbon substitutes that are nontoxic.

In lieu of petroleum-derived insulation products, wood fiber insulation is processed from wood waste products and comes in a variety of densities for interior and exterior applications. (Courtesy of TimberHP)

With advances in wood manufacturing, it is possible to turn wood waste into bio-based products. A number of wood products available today are doing just that, including wood fiber–based insulation with dense pack loose fill and batt options for cavity insulation and a rigid exterior insulation board. These have been available in Europe for several years. Most recently, Maine-based TimberHP began making these products in a closed-down paper mill. Beck, in Germany, produces wooden nails that can be used for finish and structure. The X-fix is an incredibly smart two-piece double dovetail wooden connector for wood-to-wood connection for cross-laminated timber and other mass timber elements.[13] It's almost ridiculous how many options architects and developers have at their disposal today to avoid high–embodied carbon building components. This also means it's possible to build high-quality,

low-energy midrise buildings almost completely out of wood: structure, insulation, façade, finishes, even nails and connectors! The future is decarbonized and deeply incredible.

My underdog selection for cleverest approach to decarbonizing buildings involves straw, a byproduct of grain and cereal harvests. Wheat straw is abundant, and binding it into building materials is a form of carbon sequestration that may be unsurpassed. This is because straw makes an effective insulation. Perhaps no product exemplifies the low-tech/high-tech pairing than EcoCocon's exterior straw wall solution. EcoCocon uses industrialized processes to produce structural timber–straw panels. The panels are prefabricated off-site, made to measure with 1-millimeter precision, and 1 square meter of panel stores nearly 100 kilograms of carbon dioxide, according to EcoCocon's environmental product declaration.[14] The system as a whole is incredibly elegant, resists fire for up to two hours, and is a Passive House–certified component. Prefabricated straw panels pair incredibly well with mass timber and have been deployed on numerous low-rise and even midrise buildings in Europe.

EcoCocon fabricates Passive House–certified exterior straw and wood wall panels that can be delivered to construction sites and rapidly installed. The system is stunning and may be the most underrated approach to sequestering carbon. (Credit: EcoCocon Straw Wall System)

On Carbon Offsets

A topic that has come up fairly frequently on our projects with regard to decarbonization of buildings, districts, and operations is forestry carbon offsets. Protecting forests, which continue to absorb carbon dioxide over time, has been one of the more common approaches in the United States. Unfortunately, this is also a topic where the polycrisis looms large. Wildfires in Canada and the United States have burned through many of the forests reserved for those offsets,[15] and 26 percent of existing US forests set aside for carbon offsets are at risk of wildfire.[16] This is why at Larch Lab we focus so heavily on decarbonization of the built environment *and* reduction of operation emissions through Passive House.

All of these products and strategies would have a sizable impact on reducing the embodied carbon emitted during the construction of ecodistricts. They

would make for ecological, high-quality, comfortable, and safe buildings. Unfortunately, there is substantial difficulty in realizing these projects in the United States. Construction costs are a large part. Policies could be in place to expedite the rollout of innovative products and materials, and there could be bio-based mandates, as seen in Amsterdam and France. Requiring an LCA for building permissions could also go a long way toward transparency in the built environment and nudge the industry toward widespread decarbonization.

We already have the tools, and the technology, to produce livable high-quality places with low ecological footprints. Many of these systems are also incredibly synergistic and can be paired together. With advances in work being done under entities such as the Carbon Leadership Forum, Architects Climate Action Network, New European Bauhaus, and Bauhaus der Erde (Bauhaus Earth), this focus on rehabilitation and rapid decarbonization of the built environment will only increase. We will need to find the policy levers, incentives, and mandates for our construction industry here to do the same.

These types of buildings are already viable in Europe, and they need to be viable in the United States in order to meet our climate goals. One of my favorite projects is Querbeet (Across the Board) in Lueneburg, Germany, a cohousing project for families with children, retirees, singles, and couples. This stunning project is two four-story buildings surrounding a courtyard with a mass timber structure, exterior straw walls to meet Passive House, and clay plaster finishes.[17] I have been trying to build like this on my own, and now at Larch Lab, for a decade, but the costs and processes for achieving this in the United States are prohibitive. We need to expedite buildings like this, because they will simultaneously address the housing and climate crises.

TimberHP's batt insulation is a healthy, low-carbon approach to insulating new or retrofit projects. (Credit: TimberHP)

CHAPTER 20

Futureproofing with Open Building

"We should not forecast what will happen, but try to make provisions for the unforeseen."

—N. John Habraken

The challenge to converting office buildings to residential buildings is that they were not built with the potential to adapt to other uses. Had our development regulations mandated more flexible buildings and thinner floor plates, there would be significantly more office-to-residential conversions in the postpandemic era. This lack of flexibility has instead resulted in the opposite: massive buildings unable to be adapted to other uses without extensive cost. Goldman Sachs announced that without a price drop as large as 50 percent in office buildings, developers will not be able to get these conversions to work economically.[1] This is directly related to misaligned priorities in the built environment, such as short-term profit over the ability to adapt over time as attitudes and programs shift. That lack of flexibility is unfortunately not limited to office buildings.

This inability to adapt means these buildings are effectively going to be one- or at most two-generation buildings, lacking durability and limiting long-term cohesion of neighborhoods. In its guide for buildings that last, the American Institute of Architects notes that the "primary goal of design for adaptability is to lengthen a building's lifespan by making it possible to adapt the space with minimal disruption" and that there are numerous benefits for prioritizing adaptability: reduced greenhouse gases and waste, resilient and durable buildings, and economic resilience.[2]

There are significant embodied carbon savings with adaptive transformation over demolition and new construction. This also means more wealth and labor going back into the local community instead of extractive and carbon-intensive products made elsewhere. Planning buildings and districts that are flexible and adaptive to changing needs must be a priority in the construction industry.

Open Bouwen

N. John Habraken was a Dutch architect who developed a theory about user-centered projects and flexibility in architecture, a "construction which allows the provisions of dwellings which can be built, altered and taken down independent of the others."[3] Habraken called this fixed framework or superstructure *supports*. But the infill, the interior, was something that could be altered by its residents. Habraken's work was closely connected to centering users in housing. Habraken was founding director of Stichting Architecten Research (SAR; Foundation for Architects Research), and Molenvliet, one of the first built projects using this philosophy, saw SAR engaging in private meetings with future inhabitants, incorporating their wants and needs into the home. SAR effectively tailored dwellings for residents,[4] something that is almost unheard of in multifamily housing today but very much a part of the process of planning cohousing or a Baugruppe.

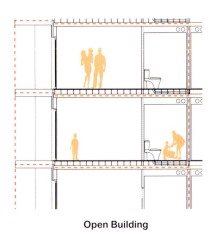 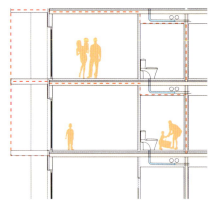

Open Building   Typical Construction

Habraken viewed the Modernist postwar architecture of the time as putting people in barracks, and the same thing could be said of housing in US cities today. Habraken's concepts of a fixed framework and flexible or adaptable interiors eventually was formalized as the open building. This resulted in development that optimized the design of a building for the long term, having fixed aspects of the development (the structure and to a larger degree the building envelope) and aspects that can be adjusted over a shorter time period (the interiors, mechanical and plumbing systems). Today, these concepts can be found in buildings all around the world. Incorporating open building principles into new buildings will ensure that space for adaptability exists. This

Diagram showing the self-contained approach of open buildings compared with typical construction practices that require dropping plumbing or other appurtenances into the soffit of the unit below. (Credit: Michael Eliason/Larch Lab)

is increasingly important in dealing with the effects of climate change. As noted in chapter 17, climate zones will migrate, perhaps significantly. Merely updating mechanical systems in existing buildings won't be adequate when the building science for these structures is completely upended with this migration. Although the movement toward open buildings is global in scope, with advocacy and projects in the United States, Japan, and China, no place has taken up Habraken's mantle more than the Netherlands, where several buildings have been completed in the last decade.[5] One of the more elegant solutions is FRANTZEN et al architecten's Patch 22, a seven-story mass timber open building in Amsterdam, designed around the idea of having a simple and flexible plan that is able to accommodate a variety of dwelling sizes or even different uses within the same development. The building's plumbing system is situated under a floating finish floor but above the structural floor and ceiling of the unit below, tying back to a central connection point.[6] This allows for future adaptability in the units without needing to enter another unit below, as would be the case in typical construction.

Straw, plaster, and wood are increasingly at the heart of circular construction and decarbonized open buildings. (Credit: Michael Burchert)

In part, open building is about disentangling systems. One particularly fascinating aspect is how mechanical, electrical, and plumbing distribution is handled. In construction in the United States, these elements (especially plumbing pipes and drains) can be found in the floor framing or under the soffit ceiling of the dwelling below the inhabited one. Open building uses a raised floor system that allows access to these systems and keeps everything contained within the inhabited dwelling. This has some interesting effects, such as increased floor thicknesses and limited runs on plumbing systems to ensure adequate drainage and flow. This approach pairs well with mass timber, discussed in chapter 18, and how floors are installed in much of

Futureproofing with Open Building 175

Europe, with insulation above the structure rather than below it. In China and Japan, there are prefabricated raised flooring systems that can also be used with this arrangement.[7]

The lifespan of buildings in Japan has historically been very low compared with other countries. With the government aiming to be carbon neutral by 2050, considerable efforts are needed to shift from the throwaway culture related to buildings and housing to one of adaptation and rehabilitation.[8] One approach has been the Act for Promotion of Long-Life Quality Housing, which the Japanese government passed in 2009. This act is intended to introduce more durable and high-quality buildings in order to reduce waste and increase the lifecycle of houses and condos through the use of special loan packages and tax benefits. Requirements for meeting this standard include energy performance, ease of maintenance and rehabilitation, and increases in seismic resistance.

In Winterthur, Switzerland, Schmidt Hammer Lassen Architects are planning Rocket & Tigerli, a flexible, mixed-use, 100-meter-tall mass timber hybrid tower. The structure incorporates two parallel load-bearing tubes, one for the stair and elevator core and the other at the exterior. These tubes are at most 23 feet apart, significantly thinner than most towers in the United States outside the pencil-thin supertalls in New York City. This thinness makes for more livable dwelling through better daylighting, but it also ensures that the building can endure downturns and changes in use.[9]

Habraken's legacy is found in the numerous innovative and adaptive buildings, often co-produced with the users, that exist around the world. And the movement is growing. It also sits at the intersection of circularity, climate adaptation, prefabrication, mass timber, building decarbonization, and new forms of living and ownership. This is the way we should be planning buildings today: flexible and easily adaptable.

EPILOGUE

Unleashing Brilliant Futures

"We are only just beginning to scratch the surface of the power of a positive vision of an abundant future: one which is energy-lean, time-rich, less stressful, healthier, and happier. Being able to associate images and a clear vision with how a powered-down future might be is essential."

—Rob Hopkins, Transition Network

The illustrations in this book include photos of built environments and drawings of proposed or yet-to-be-realized projects. This is intentional. One of the great things about architecture and planning is that a sketch or diagram can pare down to the essence of something, without getting bogged down in the minutiae. With a photograph, especially outside the disciplines of architecture and urban planning, it is easy to overlook the basic details because the arrangements and materials may be quite different. I can look at a rendering of an ecodistrict and quickly have a sense of what it might be like to live in that place. What the urban form will feel like, the rough quality of the open space. However, the sketch is not photorealistic. It is a promise not of what is to be built but what *may* be built. It leaves open numerous possibilities and potentialities. My hope is that you may also see yourself visiting, planning, or residing in places like those already built or proposed in this book.

The status quo of development in the United States and Canada is incredibly broken, with gentrification, bankruptcy, displacement, an exploding wealth gap, and increasing homelessness. It is resulting in communities that are less adaptive to a changing climate, that are not rooted in place, and that do not facilitate the transition to low-carbon living because of poor policies, infrastructure, and planning.

Despite all this, I believe things are headed in a better direction, albeit significantly slower and far less climate adaptive than necessary. The Biden administration is putting a lot of effort into housing supply and zoning reform, energy-efficient buildings, electrification, and transit. At the state level, California and Washington have passed a number of bills, and a dozen states are looking at building code reform as a tool for unlocking more family-friendly and climate adaptive housing. Massachusetts is the first state to push its energy code to meet the stringent requirements of the Passive House standard.

At the local level, there is a new type of developer looking to move beyond box-checking sustainability programs. Though lacking the open space, climate resilience, and economic and social mix of most EU ecodistricts, the Opticos-designed Culdesac development in Tempe, Arizona, is showing that there is significant demand for car-free transit-adjacent development, even in the auto-centric suburbs of the Sunbelt.[1] The first few phases of the project, located adjacent to a four-lane arterial with center-running light rail, are completed, and work on the next phases of development is continuing. The completed buildout of the 16-acre project will have about 640 homes.

In Ann Arbor, Michigan, THRIVE Collaborative's Veridian at Country Farm is pushing the limits of low-impact development with a 100 percent

Located in Tempe, Arizona, Culdesac is a car-free, mixed-use community currently under development, featuring small-scale urban forms and pedestrianized streets and passageways. (Credit: Culdesac)

solar-powered, fossil fuel–free community currently under construction. Veridian features a broad array of housing types and sizes, including studio apartments, duplexes, rowhouses, and four-bedroom homes. There is also affordable housing. Community amenities include open space, electric vehicle sharing, e–cargo bike sharing, a multifunctional barn repurposed from a nearby farm, garden tool share, and a retail space with a café and Farm Stop.[2] The Farm Stop[3] is a fascinating direct-to-consumer shop, bringing 100 percent local agricultural products to market. THRIVE's founder, Matt Grocoff, knows water and climate resilience better than any developer I have ever talked to, and he is already using the experiences and knowledge gained on this to push for denser and larger communities.

Situated on a former airfield, Downsview is a massive undertaking in Toronto that will see a climate-focused, car-light development with a capacity for 84,000 residents and 42,000 jobs. (Credit: Henning Larsen, KPMB Architects and SLA on Downsview)

In San Diego, the Neighborhood Next stadium ecodistrict is currently in planning. This car-light community will include 5,000 homes (with a quarter being affordable housing), abundant open space, connections to natural surroundings, institutional and cultural spaces, and space for commerce. That this project includes both the Copenhagen-based 3XN and Gehl on the planning team[4] leads me to believe it will probably be a beacon project in the United States.

Epilogue 179

Similarly, Toronto's Downsview airport, planned to close in 2024, will be transformed from a 520-acre brownfield to a series of dense districts, parks, and open space connected by a green spine prioritizing active transit. According to the Framework Plan,[5] ten districts would have capacity for nearly 42,00 jobs and housing for 84,000 residents, mostly at the midrise scale, with towers situated near transit stations and as accent buildings in neighborhoods. Sustainability will be central to the project, with low-carbon buildings, high-performance building envelopes, active mobility, and blue-green infrastructure integral to the urban fabric. The development group is a collaboration between Toronto-based KPMB architects, Copenhagen-based SLA Architects, and Henning Larsen Architects. The scale of the development is comparable to that of Vienna's Seestadt but with nearly four times as many residents. It is hands-down the largest, most ambitious, and most innovative redevelopment I have seen proposed for the United States and Canada, incorporating the very things I have been advocating for in the Pacific Northwest for years.

In the Bronx, Grimshaw and Dattner Architects' Via Verde cooperative for Jonathan Rose Companies, completed in 2012, showed that even at a dense,

Massing diagram for Downsview, featuring diverse neighborhoods, parks, open space, and climate adaptive elements woven throughout. (Credit: Henning Larsen, KPMB Architects and SLA on Downsview)

urban scale, these types of projects prioritizing affordability and climate adaptation are viable. We don't have to always look abroad for excellent and inclusive models.

Policy Levers

As I have attempted to lay out in this book, we have already, as a collective species, imagined these brilliant futures. We can reimagine brilliant futures, or we can work together and build the brilliant futures we have already imagined. The knowledge base for all these things already exists. The incredible number of public health benefits associated with ecodistrict developments are widely known. The technical constraints no longer bind us. What prevents these communities from flourishing is incongruity in policy and finance, and processes where those opposed to positive changes, relaxed parking requirements, and even affordable housing can stifle it.

When I spoke about these concepts at the National Association of Housing and Redevelopment Officials 2023 Summer Symposium in Washington, DC, a conference full of housers and others working in the affordable housing development and policy spheres for decades, most I talked to and interacted with were unaware of them. Much about modern urban development, and especially district-scale development, in other countries is a complete unknown to even practicing professionals on this side of the Atlantic. We have long lacked the syntax to even talk about many of these concepts, such as point access blocks. There has not been an adequate and comprehensive look at the interconnectedness of climate and livability with the dwelling, the building, the block, or the district. This book highlights what those differences and interconnections are so that the political will, the policy levers, and the financial means to achieve them can be aligned to more meaningful ends.

Enabling Impactful Futures

Avoiding carbon lock-in, meeting our climate goals, and building high-quality and livable spaces and places that can adapt to the extremes we will be seeing with climate change are not only possible but imperative. Jan Gehl famously stated, "First we shape the cities—then they shape us,"[6] and over time I have come to believe this is fundamentally true. The way we plan and build our cities and neighborhoods is directly related to the quality of the life that we allow. It directly frames what a neighborhood can be or grow into and even how it changes over time. How we plan and create new neighborhoods and districts will have a significant impact on our ability to adapt to a rapidly changing climate, fostering better community connections to reduce social isolation and loneliness and ensuring thriving economically and socially mixed places.

As Rob Hopkins states, we must have a clear vision.[7] In order for that vision to be realized, we must imagine brilliant futures. Now, *you* have the tools. *You* have the syntax and the knowledge. *You* have the ability to go forth and advocate to bring about the changes, the policies, and the designs—to enable and create these impactful communities.

It will take you, me—all of us—to create livable, low-carbon communities.

Notes

Chapter 1

1. Jean-Paule Junkers, "Speech by President Jean-Claude Juncker at the Annual General Meeting of the Hellenic Federation of Enterprises." European Commission, 2016, https://ec.europa.eu/commission/presscorner/detail/en/SPEECH_16_2293.

2. Office of the Surgeon General, "Our Epidemic of Loneliness and Isolation: The U.S. Surgeon General's Advisory on the Healing Effects of Social Connection and Community," US Department of Health and Human Services, 2023, https://www.hhs.gov/sites/default/files/surgeon-general-social-connection-advisory.pdf.

3. Robert Cervero and Cathleen Sullivan, "Green TODs: Marrying Transit-Oriented Development and Green Urbanism," *International Journal of Sustainable Development & World Ecology* 18, no. 3 (2011): 210–218, doi:10.1080/13504509.2011.570801.

4. OECD, "Compact City Policies. A Comparative Assessment," OECD Publishing, Paris, May 14, 2012.

5. Simon Joss, "Eco-Cities: The Mainstreaming of Urban Sustainability—Key Characteristics and Driving Factors," *International Journal of Sustainable Development and Planning* 6 (September 2011): 268–285, doi:10.2495/SDP-V6-N3-268-285.

6. City of Hamburg, "Leitlinien zur Lebenswerten Kompakten Stadt (Guidelines for a Livable Compact City)," September 12, 2019, https://www.hamburg.de/contentblob/13350134/80d2e53670456aab8a093e5376185933/data/d-hamburger-mass-leitlinien-zur-lebenswerten-kompakten-stadt.pdf.

7. French Ministry of Ecological Transition, "Une Nouvelle Façon de Concevoir, de Construire et de Gérer la Ville Durablement (A New Way of Designing, Building and Managing the City Sustainably)," http://www.ecoquartiers.logement.gouv.fr/.

8. EcoDistricts, "Protocol: The Global Performance Standard that Empowers Sustainable Neighborhood- and District-Scale Development," 2016, accessed October 12, 2023, https://justcommunities.info/wp-content/uploads/2016/05/ed-protocol-guide-V1-1B.pdf.

9. Capitol Hill Ecodistrict, "Our Story," accessed September 23, 2023, https://www.capitolhillecodistrict.org/our-story.

10. Just Communities, "EcoDistricts Acquisition FAQ," Partnership for Southern Equity, accessed October 12, 2023, https://justcommunities.info/frequently-asked-questions.

11. Projektgruppe Dietenbach, "Dietenbach Städtebaulicher Rahmenplan | Erläuterungsbericht (Dietenbach Urban Development Framework Plan | Explanatory Report)," Stadt Freiburg im Breisgau, November 2020, https://www.freiburg.de/pb/site/Freiburg/get/params_E1438575820/1632097/G_20094_Anlage_2_Dietenbach_Rahmenplan_Erl%C3%A4uterungsbericht.pdf.

12. Proposal to update the development goals for Dietenbach as a guideline for the development approval of property purchase agreements.

13. Meta Berghauser Pont and Per Haupt, "The Relation between Urban Form and Density," *Urban Morphology* 11 (April 2007): 62–65.

14. Peter Andreas Sattrup and Jakob Strømann-Andersen, "Building Typologies in Northern European Cities: Daylight, Solar Access, and Building Energy Use," *Journal of Architectural and Planning Research* 30 (2013).

15. Philipp Rode, Pablo Viejo Garcia, et al., " Cities and Energy Urban Morphology and Heat Energy Demand," LSE Cities, London, March 2014, https://www.lse.ac.uk/cities/publications/research-reports/Cities-and-Energy.

16. Bengt Sundborg, Barbara Matusiak, and Shabnam Arbab, "Perimeter Blocks in Different Forms: Aspects of Daylight and View," *IOP Conference Series: Earth and Environmental Science* 323 (2019), doi:10.1088/1755-1315/323/1/012153.

17. Brent Toderian, "Toderian: Density Done Well," *Spacing Magazine*, April 10, 2013, http://spacing.ca/national/2013/04/10/toderian-density-done-well.

Chapter 2

1. Ainslie Cruickshank, "Clark Dr. Pollution Shows Pitfalls of Building More Homes along Busy Roads," *Toronto Star*,

February 12, 2019, https://www.thestar.com/vancouver/clark-dr-pollution-shows-pitfalls-of-building-more-homes-along-busy-roads/article_509733b9-0df2-570c-9f52-ee7dcab3faad.html.

2. Emily Badger and Quoctrung Bui, "Cities Start to Question an American Ideal: A House With a Yard on Every Lot," *New York Times*, June 18, 2019, https://www.nytimes.com/interactive/2019/06/18/upshot/cities-across-america-question-single-family-zoning.html.

3. Daniel Parolek, "What Is Missing Middle Housing?," Missing Middle Housing, https://missingmiddlehousing.com/about.

4. Peter Calthorpe, *The Next American Metropolis: Ecology, Community, and the American Dream* (New York: Princeton Architectural Press, 1993).

5. Center for Neighborhood Technology, "TOD Database," https://cnt.org/tools/tod-database.

6. Brenda Scheer et al., "How Does Transportation Affordability Vary among TODs, TADs, and Other Areas?," National Institute for Transportation and Communities, August 2017, https://rosap.ntl.bts.gov/view/dot/35375.

7. Mariia Zimmermann, "Parking: A Major Barrier to Equitably Oriented Transit," Strong-Prosperous and Resilient Communities Challenge, February 2020, https://www.sparcchub.org/wp-content/uploads/2020/02/Parking-A-Major-Barrier-to-Equitably-Oriented-Transit.pdf.

8. Laura Bliss, "Utah's Walkable '15-Minute City' Could Still Leave Lots of Room for Cars," Bloomberg, March 21, 2022, accessed November 23, 2023, https://www.bloomberg.com/news/articles/2022-03-21/utah-dreams-up-a-different-kind-of-15-minute-city.

9. Fang Bian, SI Qiao, and Anthony Yeh, "Mobility Resilience: Transit-Oriented Development, Ride-Hailing, and Car Ownership," *Transportation Research Part D Transport and Environment* 123 (October 2023), doi:10.1016/j.trd.2023.103924.

10. Mark Swilling et al., "The Weight of Cities: Resource Requirements of Future Urbanization," a report by the International Resource Panel, United Nations Environment Programme, 2018, https://www.resourcepanel.org/reports/weight-cities.

11. Institute for Transportation & Development Policy, "TOD Standard," 2017, https://www.itdp.org/publication/tod-standard/.

12. Intergovernmental Panel on Climate Change (IPCC), ed., "Urban Systems and Other Settlements," chapter in *Climate Change 2022—Mitigation of Climate Change: Working Group III Contribution to the Sixth Assessment Report of the Intergovernmental Panel on Climate Change*, 927 (Cambridge, UK: Cambridge University Press, 2023).

13. Peter Erickson and Kevin Tempest, "Keeping Cities Green: Avoiding Carbon Lock-in Due to Urban Development," Stockholm Environment Institute, 2015.

Chapter 3

1. Sarah De Boeck and Michael Ryckewaert, "The Preservation of Productive Activities in Brussels: The Interplay between Zoning and Industrial Gentrification," *Urban Planning* 5 (2020): doi:10.17645/up.v5i3.3092.

2. McKinsey & Company, "What Are Industry 4.0, the Fourth Industrial Revolution, and 4IR?," August 17, 2022, https://www.mckinsey.com/featured-insights/mckinsey-explainers/what-are-industry-4-0-the-fourth-industrial-revolution-and-4ir#/.

3. European Commission, "New Leipzig Charter—The Transformative Power of Cities for the Common Good," November 30, 2020, https://ec.europa.eu/regional_policy/en/information/publications/brochures/2020/new-leipzig-charter-the-transformative-power-of-cities-for-the-common-good.

4. Municipal Department 18, Urban Development and Urban Planning, "STEP 2025 Fachkonzept Produktive Stadt (STEP 2025 Technical Subject Productive City)," City of Vienna, 2017, https://www.wien.gv.at/stadtentwicklung/strategien/step/step2025/fachkonzepte/fachkonzept-produktive-stadt.html.

5. Edeltraud Haselsteiner et al., "VERTICALurbanFACTORY Innovative Konzepte der vertikalen Verdichtung von Produktion und Stadt (VERTICALurbanFACTORY Innovative Concepts for the Vertical Densification of Production and the City)," Federal Ministry for Climate Action, Environment, Energy, Mobility, Innovation and Technology (BMK), August 2019, https://nachhaltigwirtschaften.at/resources/sdz_pdf/schriftenreihe-2020-9b-verticalurbanfactory.pdf.

6. Emmanuelle Borne, "Projet: Bruxelles, Ville Productive," *L'Architecture d'Aujourd'hui*, 430 (May 2019): 72.

7. Bouwmeester Maitre Architecte, "Brussels Productive City," City of Brussels, June 2019, https://bma.brussels/en/something-productive/.

8. Julie Baumgardner, "New Lab's Co-Working Space Is an Antidote to the Rent-a-Desk Model That's Sweeping the Globe," *Wallpaper*, October 20, 2020, https://www.wallpaper.com/architecture/new-lab-coworking-space-in-brooklyn-navy-yard.

9. Office of Planning & Community Development, "Seattle's Industrial and Maritime Strategy—Director's Report and Recommendation" City of Seattle, March 2023, https://www.seattle.gov/documents/Departments/OPCD/OngoingInitiatives/IndustrialMaritimeStrategy/IndustrialMaritimeFinalDirectorsReport2023.pdf.

10. Workshop East, "Co-Making: Research into London's Open Access Makerspaces and Shared Workshops," London Legacy Development Corporation and the Greater London Authority, January 2015, https://www.london.gov.uk/sites/default/files/makerspaces-jan2015.pdf

11. Nina Rappaport, *Vertical Urban Factories* (Barcelona: Actar Publishing, August 15, 2016): 416–417.

12. Tom Assmann et al., "Planung von Lastenradumschlagsknoten—Planungsleitfaden (Planning of Cargo Bike Delivery Nodes—Planning Guide)," Otto-von-Guericke-Universität Magdeburg, Oktober 2019, https://www.ilm.ovgu.de/Planungsleitfaden_Lastenrad.html.

13. JOTT architekten and urbanism et al., "Produktives Stadtquartier Winnenden Städtebaulicher Rahmenplan (Productive Urban District of Winnenden Urban Development Plan)," City of Winnenden, December 15, 2021, https://www.winnenden.de/start/bauen-umwelt/iba.html.

14. Statistics Vienna, "Vienna in Figures 2022," City of Vienna, August 2022, https://www.wien.gv.at/statistik/pdf/viennainfigures-2022.pdf.

15. Eléna Seitaridis, "Freunde von Freunden," April 14, 2016, https://www.friendsoffriends.com/features/coffee-grown-mushrooms-and-other-feats-of-urban-production-in-vienna.

16. Francesco Bassetti, "Can Urban Farming Play a Key Role in Food Security?," *The Japan Times*, March 6, 2023, https://www.japantimes.co.jp/life/2023/03/06/environment/japan-urban-farming.

Chapter 4

1. Bullitt Center, "Net Positive Energy over First Decade," April 20, 2023, https://bullittcenter.org/2023/04/20/net-positive-energy-over-first-decade.

2. Vignesh Ramasamy et al., "U.S. Solar Photovoltaic System and Energy Storage Cost Benchmarks, with Minimum Sustainable Price Analysis: Q1 2023," National Renewable Energy Laboratory, September 2023, https://www.nrel.gov/docs/fy23osti/87303.pdf.

3. Matthias Arning, Christiane Krämer, and Alexander Noller, "Wohnen im Aktiv-Stadthaus (Living in the Active Townhouse),"ABG Frankfurt Holding, June 2015, https://www.abgnova.de/pdf/2015_PDF/Broschuere_Aktiv-Stadthaus_Juni_2015_WEB.pdf.

4. Public Relations Department, "Die Bahnstadt Ihr Platz am Wissenschaftsstandort Heidelberg (Bahnstadt Your Place at the Science Center Heidelberg)," City of Heidelberg, September 2019, https://www.heidelberg-bahnstadt.de/site/HD_Satelliten/get/documents_E-446766346/heidelberg/Objektdatenbank/Bahnstadt/heidelberg-bahnstadt.de/Pdf/190927_Brosch%C3%BCre_Bahnstadt_final.pdf.

5. Søren Peper, "Energy Monitoring of Residential Buildings in the Passive House City District of Heidelberg-Bahnstadt," Passive House Institute, October 2016, https://passiv.de/downloads/05_heidelberg_bahnstadt_monitoring_report_en.pdf.

6. Karine Lacroix et al., "Different Names for 'Natural Gas' Influence Public Perception of It," *Journal of Environmental Psychology* 77 (October 2021), doi:10.1016/j.jenvp.2021.101671.

7. Rebecca Leber, "How the Fossil Fuel Industry Convinced Americans to Love Gas Stoves and Why They're Scared We Might Break Up with Their Favorite Appliance," *Mother Jones*, June 17, 2021, https://www.motherjones.com/environment/2021/06/how-the-fossil-fuel-industry-convinced-americans-to-love-gas-stoves.

8. Environmental Protection Agency, "Basic Information about NO_2," updated July 25, 2023, https://www.epa.gov/no2-pollution/basic-information-about-no2.

9. Taylor Gruenwald et al., "Population Attributable Fraction of Gas Stoves and Childhood Asthma in the United States," *International Journal of Environmental Research and Public Health* 20, no. 1 (2023): 75, doi:10.3390/ijerph20010075.

10. Melissa Clark, "The Case for Induction Cooking, versus Gas Stoves," *The New York Times*, March 11, 2022, https://www.nytimes.com/2022/03/11/dining/induction-cooking.html.

11. Caroline Mimbs Nyce, "J. Kenji López-Alt Thinks You'll Be Fine with an Induction Stove," *The Atlantic*, January 31, 2023, https://www.theatlantic.com/ideas/archive/2023/01/j-kenji-lopez-alt-induction-gas-stove-electric-coil/672897/.

12. Federal Energy Regulatory Commission, "Inquiry into Bulk-Power System Operations During December 2022 Winter Storm Elliott," October 2023, https://www.ferc.gov/news-events/news/ferc-nerc-release-final-report-lessons-winter-storm-elliott.

13. Andrew Weber and Mose Buchele, "An Austin Woman Died from Hypothermia during the Blackout. Four Months Later, Her Husband Died, Too," KUT, August 4, 2022, https://www.kut.org/health/2022-08-04/shah-family-lost-power-austin-2021-winter-storm.

14. Small Planet Supply, "Drop-In Central DHW Plant Systems for Multifamily or Commercial Projects," https://www.smallplanetsupply.com/waterdrop.

15. Jan Rosenow et al., "Heating Up the Global Heat Pump Market," *Nature Energy* 7 (2022): 901–904, doi:10.1038/s41560-022-01104-8.

16. Markus Zahno and Christoph Albrecht, "Hier entsteht das Quartier der Zukunft (The Quarter of the Future Is Being

Built Here)," *Berner Zeitung*, January 22, 2019, https://www.bernerzeitung.ch/hier-entsteht-das-quartier-der-zukunft-516114337192.

17. Petra Schöfmann et al., "Zukunftsquartier 2.0 Replizierbare, thermisch und elektrisch netzdienliche Konzeption von (Plus-Energie-) Quartieren im dichten urbanen Kontext (Future Quarter 2.0 Replicable, Thermally and Electrical Grid-Friendly Conception of (Plus-Energy) Quarters in a Dense Urban Context)," Ministry of Climate Action and Energy, May 2022, https://nachhaltigwirtschaften.at/resources/sdz_pdf/schriftenreihe-2023-33-zukunftsquartier-2-0.pdf.

Chapter 5

1. Center for Building in North America, "Single-Stair Reform Efforts across North America," https://www.centerforbuilding.org/singlestair-tracker.

2. Litic Murali, "2020 Multifamily Completion Data: Property Size," NAHB Eye on Housing, August 16, 2021, https://eyeonhousing.org/2021/08/2020-multifamily-completion-data-property-size.

3. Anna Kodé, "America, the Bland," *New York Times*, January 20, 2023, https://www.nytimes.com/2023/01/20/realestate/housing-developments-city-architecture.html.

4. Emily Badger et al., "The Housing Shortage Isn't Just a Coastal Crisis Anymore," *New York Times*, July 14, 2022, https://www.nytimes.com/2022/07/14/upshot/housing-shortage-us.html.

5. Stephen Smith, "Why We Can't Build Family-Sized Apartments in North America," Center for Building in North America, May 4, 2023, https://www.centerforbuilding.org/blog/we-we-cant-build-family-sized-apartments-in-north-america.

6. Michael Gove, "Long-Term Plan for Housing: Secretary of State's Speech," London, UK, Department for Levelling Up, Housing and Communities, 2023, https://www.gov.uk/government/speeches/long-term-plan-for-housing-secretary-of-states-speech.

7. European Fire Sprinkler Network, "B.I.O. Summary of Legislative Incentives for Fire Sprinklers in New Buildings," 2022, https://www.eurosprinkler.org/wp-content/uploads/2022/07/Summary-Legislation.pdf.

8. Conrad Speckert, "The Second Egress: Building a Code Change," accessed October 12, 2023, https://secondegress.ca.

Chapter 6

1. Jerusalem Demsas, "Community Input Is Bad, Actually," *The Atlantic*, April 22, 2022, https://www.theatlantic.com/ideas/archive/2022/04/local-government-community-input-housing-public-transportation/629625/.

2. Chris Maddox, "Why the RFP Is the Enemy of Innovation," *Governing*, January 25, 2017, https://www.governing.com/gov-institute/voices/col-technology-startups-rfp-enemy-innovation.html.

3. Francesca Gina, "3 Strategies for Making Better, More Informed Decisions," *Harvard Business Review*, May 25, 2023, https://hbr.org/2023/05/3-strategies-for-making-better-more-informed-decisions.

4. European Union, "Directive 2004/18/EC of the European Parliament and of the Council," March 31, 2004, https://eur-lex.europa.eu/legal-content/EN/TXT/HTML/?uri=CELEX:32004L0018.

5. "Architectural Design Competitions: A Key Policy Tool to Ensure Quality in the Built Environment," October 25, 2019, https://www.ace-cae.eu/practice-of-the-profession/architectural-design-competitions-adc/the-ace-uia-statement/.

6. European Parliament, "European Parliament—Paul-Henri SPAAK Building Brussels," https://www.european-parliament-design-competition.eu/projects_european-parliament-design-competition_home.htm.

7. Architekturfestival TURN ON, "Kristiaan Borret, Stadbaumeister Bruessels," March 9, 2018, 16:12, https://www.youtube.com/watch?v=vHt7XLtsLTw.

8. Stadt Köln, "Wettbewerb Max Becker-Areal: Ein neues Stadtquartier für Köln (Competition Max Becker Area: A New City Quarter for Cologne)," October 2022, https://www.stadt-koeln.de/mediaasset/content/pdf61/max-becker-areal_dokumentation_wettbewerb.pdf.

9. Henning Larsen, "Fælledby," https://henninglarsen.com/en/projects/featured/1915-faelledby/.

10. Kirchheim Unter Teck, "Das Steingauquartier: Information Handout 1," April 3, 2018, https://www.kirchheim-teck.de/ceasy/resource/?id=12899&download=1.

11. Thomas Gauggel and Matthias Guetschow, "Kommunale Grundstücksvergabe: Offene Konzeptvergabe in der Stadtentwicklung (Municipal Land Allocation: Open Concept Allocation in Urban Development)," *Quartier*, June 2022, https://www.magazin-quartier.de/article/kommunale-grundstuecksvergabe-offene-konzeptvergabe-stadtentwicklung/.

12. Gernot Pohl, "Steingauquartier—Kirchheim unter Teck," Föreningen för Byggemenskaper Conference, April 5, 2019, https://byggemenskap.se/wp-content/uploads/6.-Steingauquartier_Gernot-Pohl.pdf.

13. Robert Temel, "Concept Tendering Procedures," United Nations Human Settlements Programme, 2020, https://urbanmaestro.org/example/konzeptvergabe.

14. Enterprise Community Partners, "Home & Hope Mapping Tool," https://www.enterprisecommunity.org/about

/where-we-work/pacific-northwest/home-and-hope-mapping-tool.

15. Erwin Van der Krabben, "Private–Private Cooperation in Urban Redevelopment Projects," FIG Conference, 2014, http://www.fig.net/resources/proceedings/fig_proceedings/fig2014/papers/ts08f/TS08F_van_der_krabben_7056.pdf.

16. City of Zurich, "Stadtklimatische Anliegen in städtischen Hochbauten (Urban Climate Concerns in Urban Buildings)," August 2020, https://www.stadt-zuerich.ch/hbd/de/index/hochbau/bauen-fuer-2000-watt/grundlagen-studien ergebnisse/2020-08-nb-stadtklimatische-anliegen.html.

17. IBA Hamburg GmbH, "Project Progress," https://www.iba-hamburg.de/en/projects/oberbillwerder/project-progress.

Chapter 7

1. Francesca Palmia et al., "Enabling Meaningful Public Participation in Spatial Planning Processes," United Nations Human Settlements Programme, 2023, https://unhabitat.org/sites/default/files/2023/01/final_enabling_meaningful_public_participation_in_spatial_planning_processes.pdf.

2. Nicole Armos et al., "Beyond Inclusion: Equity in Public Engagement," Simon Fraser University's Morris J. Wosk Centre for Dialogue, 2020, https://www.sfu.ca/dialogue/resources/public-participation-and-government-decision-making/beyond-inclusion.html.

3. Brian McCabe, "When Property Values Rule," *Contexts* 13, no. 1 (2014): 38–43, doi:10.1177/1536504214522007.

4. Ray Dubicki, "Neighborhood Plans Are High-Minded Gatekeeping," *The Urbanist*, February 25, 2022, https://www.theurbanist.org/2022/02/25/neighborhood-plans-are-high-minded-gatekeeping.

5. Will James, "'Bootcamps' Aim to Educate Seattle Renters about Their Rights," KNKX, January 11, 2017, https://www.knkx.org/news/2017-01-11/bootcamps-aim-to-educate-seattle-renters-about-their-rights.

6. Lyndall Crisp, "Urban Density in a Green World," *Australian Business Review*, April 19, 2013.

7. Alana Semuels, "Highways Destroyed America's Cities," *The Atlantic*, November 25, 2015, https://www.theatlantic.com/business/archive/2015/11/highways-destroyed-americas-cities/417789.

8. Iris Kunze and Andrea Philipp, "The Eco-District of Vauban and the Co-Housing Project GENOVA," Case study report: Cohousing, TRANSIT: EU SSH.203.3.2-1, April 9 2016, http://www.transitsocialinnovation.eu/content/original/Book%20covers/Local%20PDFs/208%20Chpt%20 cohousing_vauban_2015_01_26_report_ik_ap_publication_transit.pdf.

9. Byeongsun Ahn and Elisabetta Mocca, "Unlocking the Door of the City Hall: Vienna's Participatory Shift in Urban Development Policy." *Vienna in Transition: Still a Just City?* ed. Yuri Kazepov and Roland Verwiebe (New York, Routledge, 2021): 42.

10. IBA Hamburg GmbH, "Format IBA," https://www.internationale-bauausstellung-hamburg.de/en/story/format-iba.html.

11. IBA Hamburg GmbH, "Beteiligung (Participation)," https://www.iba-hamburg.de/de/themen/beteiligung.

12. IBA Hamburg GmbH," Oberbillwerder: Project Progress," https://www.iba-hamburg.de/en/projects/oberbillwerder/project-progress.

13. Erica Barnett, "How Seattle's Well-Intentioned Planning Experiment Went Wrong," *Next City*, January 19, 2017, https://nextcity.org/urbanist-news/seattles-community-planning-experiment-fell-short.

14. Danielle Berstrom et al., "The Community Engagement Guide for Sustainable Communities," PolicyLink, 2012, https://www.policylink.org/resources-tools/community-engagement-guide-for-sustainable-communities.

15. Vienna City Administration, "The Vienna Children and Youth Strategy 2020–2025," June 2020, https://junges.wien.gv.at/wp-content/uploads/sites/48/2020/09/The-Vienna-Children-and-Youth-Strategy.pdf.

Chapter 8

1. Prof. Carlos Moreno, interview with C40 Cities, "Interview with Prof Carlos Moreno, Sustainable Design and Urban Planning Expert," C40 Cities, June 29, 2023, https://www.c40.org/news/interview-with-prof-carlos-moreno-sustainable-design-and-urban-planning-expert/.

2. Bureau of Transportation Statistics, https://data.bts.gov/Research-and-Statistics/Trips-by-Distance/w96p-f2qv/about_data.

3. Federal Highway Administration, "Data Extraction Toolkit," 2009 NHTS, https://nhts.ornl.gov/det/Extraction3.aspx.

4. Bureau of Transportation Statistics, "2019 Trips by Distance," accessed October 21, 2023, https://data.bts.gov/Research-and-Statistics/Trips-by-Distance/w96p-f2qv/about_data.

5. International Energy Agency, "Global SUV Sales Set Another Record in 2021, Setting Back Efforts to Reduce Emissions," December 21, 2021, https://www.iea.org/commentaries/global-suv-sales-set-another-record-in-2021-setting-back-efforts-to-reduce-emissions.

6. Tesla, "Model 3 Specifications," accessed October 21, 2023, https://www.tesla.com/model3.

7. Ezra Dyer, "Tested: 2022 GMC Hummer EV Edition 1

Pickup Breaks Barriers," *Car and Driver*, July 15, 2022, https://www.caranddriver.com/reviews/a40618071/2022-gmc-hummer-ev-pickup-edition-1-by-the-numbers/.

8. Drew Dorian, "2023 Honda Accord / Accord Hybrid," *Car and Driver*, 2023, accessed October 21, 2023, https://www.caranddriver.com/honda/accord-2023.

9. Amanda Holpuch, "U.S. Pedestrian Deaths Are at Highest Level in 41 Years, Report Says," *New York Times*, June 27, 2023, https://www.nytimes.com/2023/06/27/us/pedestrian-deaths-2022.html.

10. Insurance Institute for Highway Safety, "Vehicles with Higher, More Vertical Front Ends Pose Greater Risk to Pedestrians," November 14, 2023, https://www.iihs.org/news/detail/vehicles-with-higher-more-vertical-front-ends-pose-greater-risk-to-pedestrians.

11. Sandra India-Aldana, "Long-Term Exposure to Walkable Residential Neighborhoods and Risk of Obesity-Related Cancer in the New York University Women's Health Study (NYUWHS)," *Environmental Health Perspectives* 131, no. 10, October 4, 2023, https://ehp.niehs.nih.gov/doi/full/10.1289/EHP11538.

12. City of Freiburg, "Neuer Stadtteil Dietenbach—Leben in Dietenbach (New Dietenbach District—Living in Dietenbach)," https://www.freiburg.de/pb/2152276.html.

13. Andrew van Dam, "The School Bus Is Disappearing. Welcome to the Era of the School Pickup Line," *The Washington Post*, February 2, 2023, https://www.washingtonpost.com/business/2024/02/02/school-bus-era-ends.

14. City of Vienna, "Handbuch Gender Mainstreaming in der Stadtplanung und Stadtentwicklung (Handbook Gender Mainstreaming in Urban Planning and Urban Development)," 2013, https://www.wien.gv.at/stadtentwicklung/studien/b008290.html.

15. Paula Kuss and Kimberly A. Nicholas, "A Dozen Effective Interventions to Reduce Car Use in European Cities: Lessons Learned from a Meta-Analysis and Transition Management," *Case Studies on Transport Policy* 10, no. 3 (September 2022): 1494–1513, doi:10.1016/j.cstp.2022.02.001.

16. Tim Leving, "The Incredible, Earth-Saving Electric Bike Is Having a Moment," *Business Insider*, May 24, 2023, https://www.businessinsider.com/electric-bikes-popularity-sustainability-evs-2023-4.

17. Susanne Wrighton and Karl Reiter, "CycleLogistics: Moving Europe Forward!," *Transportation Research Procedia* 12 (2016): 950–958, doi:10.1016/j.trpro.2016.02.046.

18. Ersilia Verlinghieri et al., "The Promise of Low-Carbon Freight," August 2021, https://www.westminster.ac.uk/news/using-cargo-bikes-for-deliveries-cuts-congestion-and-pollution-in-cities-study-finds.

19. Aspern Development AG, "Mit dem Rad (With the Bike)," accessed November 8, 2023, https://www.aspern-seestadt.at/lebenswelt/mobilitaet/mit_dem_rad.

20. Volkswagen, "New Logistics Concept for the ID.3," October 19, 2020, https://www.glaesernemanufaktur.de/de/news-ergebnisseite/logisitkkonzept-id3.html.

21. Ralf Euler, "Das Paket kommt mit der Straßenbahn (The Package Arrives by Tram)," *Frankfurter Allgemeine Zeitung*, June 12, 2020, https://www.faz.net/aktuell/rhein-main/frankfurt/pilotversuch-in-frankfurt-das-paket-mit-der-strassenbahn-16810185.html.

22. IBA Hamburg GmbH, "Der Masterplan: Die Grundlage für Hamburgs 105. Stadtteil (The Masterplan: The Basis for Hamburgs's 105th District)," accessed October 23, 2023, https://www.oberbillwerder-hamburg.de/projekt/masterplan-2022/.

23. Wiener Linien (Vienna Transit), "WienMobil Auto: The Car Sharing Offer from Wiener Linien," accessed on September 12, 2023, https://www.wienerlinien.at/wienmobil/auto.

24. Monica Nickelsburg, "Car-Sharing Is Back in Seattle—Kind of: Envoy Launches New Electric Service at Residential Buildings," *Geekwire*, February 7, 2020, https://www.geekwire.com/2020/car-sharing-back-seattle-kind-envoy-launches-new-community-based-service-residential-buildings/.

25. Georg Dunkel, "Mobilitätskonzept Freiham Nord (Mobility Concepts Freiham North)," Lecture Muenchen Unterwegs, Munich, July 23, 2022, https://stadt.muenchen.de/dam/jcr:92016344-f635-4b97-a514-e6af1bf52b09/Praesentation_Mobilitaetskonzept.pdf.

26. NACTO, "Shared Micromobility in 2022," accessed September 19, 2023, https://nacto.org/publication/shared-micromobility-in-2022/.

27. Joshuah K. Stolaroff et al., "Energy Use and Life Cycle Greenhouse Gas Emissions of Drones for Commercial Package Delivery," *Nature Communications* 9, no. 409 (February 13, 2018), doi:10.1038/s41467-017-02411-5.

28. Andrea Gonzales and Daniel Ranostaj, "The State of Parking," Gensler, 2018, accessed November 12, 2023, https://www.gensler.com/doc/research-the-state-of-parking.pdf.

29. JaJa Architects, "Wooden Parking House Aarhus and Mobility Hub," 2019, accessed October 23, 2023 https://jaja.archi/project/wooden-parking-house-aarhus/.

Chapter 9

1. OECD, "Social Housing: A Key Part of Past and Future Housing Policy," OECD, Paris, 2020, http://oe.cd/social-housing-2020.

2. City of Vienna, "Hintergrund: Gemeindebau und Sozialer

Wohnbau in Wien (Background: Municipal and Social Housing in Vienna)," https://presse.wien.gv.at/hintergrund/wohnbau.

3. Wohnfonds_Wien, "Beurteilung (Assessment)," City of Vienna, August 2019, https://www.wohnfonds.wien.at/btw_beurteilung.

4. Paris & Métropole Aménagement, "Clichy-Batignolles (Paris 17th): A New Urban Quality for Northwest Paris," https://www.parisetmetropole-amenagement.fr/en/clichy-batignolles-paris-17th.

5. Tegel Projekt GmbH, "Building & Living," https://schumacher-quartier.de/en/building-living/.

6. Frank Maier-Solgk, "Soziale Mischung oder Abgrenzung? Neubauquartiere in Deutschland (Social Mix or Separation? New Districts in Germany)," *Bauwelt* 48 (2012): https://www.bauwelt.de/themen/bauten/Soziale-Mischung-oder-Abgrenzung-Neubauquartiere-in-Deutschland-2154739.html.

7. Österreichischer Rundfunk (Austrian Broadcasting), "Wohnbau: Zwei Drittel müssen gefördert sein (Housing: Two Thirds Must Be Subsidized)," November 5, 2018, https://wien.orf.at/v2/news/stories/2945439/.

8. Center for Disease Control and Prevention, "Disability Impacts All of Us," https://www.cdc.gov/ncbddd/disabilityandhealth/infographic-disability-impacts-all.html.

9. Luke Bo'sher et al., "Accessibility of America's Housing Stock: Analysis of the 2011 American Housing Survey (AHS)," *SSRN Electronic Journal*, March 19, 2015, doi:10.2139/ssrn.3055191.

10. Gina Schaak et al., "Priced Out: the Housing Crisis for People with Disabilities," Technical Assistance Collaborative, Inc., December 2017, https://www.tacinc.org/wp-content/uploads/2020/04/priced-out-in-2016.pdf.

11. Erick Mikiten, "Inclusive Design Standards," *The Kelsey*, September 2023, https://thekelsey.org/learn-center/design-standards.

12. Anna Patrick, "King County Reports Largest Number of Homeless People Ever," *The Seattle Times*, May 15, 2024, https://www.seattletimes.com/seattle-news/homeless/king-county-reports-largest-number-of-homeless-people-ever/.

13. Anna Patrick, "Initiative 135, Seattle 'Social Housing' Ballot Measure, Leads on Election Night," *The Seattle Times*, February 14, 2023, https://www.seattletimes.com/seattle-news/homeless/initiative-135-seattle-social-housing-ballot-measure-leads-on-election-night/.

14. Jesse Franz, "Meet the 13 People Appointed to Bring Social Housing to Seattle," *Seattle City Council Blog*, April 28, 2023, https://council.seattle.gov/2023/04/28/meet-the-13-people-appointed-to-bring-social-housing-to-seattle/.

Chapter 10

1. Christian Dimmer et al., "Privately Owned Public Space: The International," *SUR—Sustainable Urban Regeneration* 25 (2013).

2. Alex Schultz, "Owners of Vacant SF Building: 'Simply Unreasonable' to Keep Public Space Open," *SFGATE*, May 22, 2023, https://www.sfgate.com/local/article/building-owners-squabble-over-sf-public-spaces-18000504.php.

3. YEWO, "Bloch-Bauer-Promenade," https://www.yewo.at/projekt/bloch-bauer-promenade/.

4. Quartier am Rotweg, "Siegerentwurf (Winning Entry)," https://www.quartier-am-rotweg.de/iba27-neubauquartier/siegerentwurf/.

5. Karissa Rosenfield, "K + S Selected to Design New 'Skärvet' Neighborhood in Växjö," *Arch Daily*, October 19, 2014, https://www.archdaily.com/558828/k-s-selected-to-design-new-skarvet-neighborhood-in-vaxjo.

6. The Innovation in Politics Institute, "Cool Streets," https://innovationinpolitics.eu/showroom/project/cool-streets/.

Chapter 11

1. Carolina Aragão et al., "The Modern American Family," Pew Research Center, September 14, 2023, https://www.pewresearch.org/social-trends/2023/09/14/the-modern-american-family.

2. Paulina Cachero and Claire Ballentine, "Nearly Half of All Young Adults Live with Mom and Dad—and They Like It," Bloomberg, September 20, 2023, https://www.bloomberg.com/news/articles/2023-09-20/nearly-half-of-young-adults-are-living-back-home-with-parents.

3. Arnab Chakraborty and Andrew McMillan, "Is Housing Diversity Good for Community Stability? Evidence from the Housing Crisis," *Journal of Planning Education and Research* (2022), doi:10.1177/0739456X18810787.

4. Joint Center for Housing Studies of Harvard University, "Housing America's Older Adults," 2023, https://www.jchs.harvard.edu/sites/default/files/reports/files/Harvard_JCHS_Housing_Americas_Older_Adults_2023.pdf.

5. TED Talks, "How Cohousing Can Make Us Happier (and Live Longer) | Grace Kim," Vancouver, August 7, 2017, https://www.youtube.com/watch?v=mguvTfAw4wk.

6. Eastern Village Cohousing, "Cohousing: An Intro & a Journey," a presentation by Daisy Birch, August 20, 2022, https://www.youtube.com/watch?v=MZeriZOpIYk.

7. Stephen Smith, "Revealed: Haus at 152 Freeman Street, Greenpoint Passive House Baugruppe," *New York YIMBY*, November 5, 2014, https://newyorkyimby.com/2014/11/revealed-haus-at-152-freeman-street-greenpoint-passive-house-baugruppe.html.

8. The Federal Institute for Research on Building, Urban

Affairs and Spatial Development, "Clusterwohnungen: Eine neue Wohnungstypologie für eine anpassungsfähige Stadtentwicklung [Cluster Apartments: A New Housing Typology for Adaptable Urban Development]," 2020, https://www.bbsr.bund.de/BBSR/DE/veroeffentlichungen/zukunft-bauen-fp/2020/band-22.html.

9. Paul Knüsel and Jutta Glanzmann, "Mehr als Wohnen von der Brache zum Stadtquartier (More than Living from the Wasteland to the City District)," Bundesamt für Wohnungswesen BWO/Federal Office of Housing, January 27, 2016, https://www.bwo.admin.ch/bwo/de/home/wie-wir-wohnen/studien-und-publikationen/mehr-als-wohnen---von-der-brache-zum-stadtquartier.html.

10. Stadt Zuerich, "Mietpreise in der Stadt Zürich (Rent Prices in the City of Zurich)," accessed on October 14, 2023, https://www.stadt-zuerich.ch/prd/de/index/statistik/publikationen-angebote/publikationen/webartikel/2022-11-03_Mietpreise-in-der-Stadt-Zuerich.html.

11. Sydney Page, "These Single-Mom Friends Joked about Buying a House Together. On a Whim, They Did It," *The Washington Post*, March 17, 2022, https://www.washingtonpost.com/lifestyle/2022/03/17/single-moms-share-house-maryland.

12. Mietshaeuser Syndikat, "Projekte," accessed November 24, 2023, https://www.syndikat.org/projekte.

13. GLS Bank, "Mietshaeuser Syndikat," June 2016, accessed October 10, 2023, https://www.gls.de/privatkunden/wo-wirkt-mein-geld/wohnen/mietshaeuser-syndikat.

14. Julia Gilgoff, "Giving Tenants the First Opportunity to Purchase Their Homes," Shelterforce, July 24, 2020, https://shelterforce.org/2020/07/24/giving-tenants-the-first-opportunity-to-purchase-their-homes.

15. L. F. Cabeza, Q. Bai, P. Bertoldi, J. M. Kihila, A. F. P. Lucena, É. Mata, S. Mirasgedis, A. Novikova, and Y. Saheb, "Buildings," in *IPCC, 2022: Climate Change 2022: Mitigation of Climate Change. Contribution of Working Group III to the Sixth Assessment Report of the Intergovernmental Panel on Climate Change*, ed. P. R. Shukla, J. Skea, R. Slade, A. Al Khourdajie, R. van Diemen, D. McCollum, M. Pathak, S. Some, P. Vyas, R. Fradera, M. Belkacemi, A. Hasija, G. Lisboa, S. Luz, and J. Malley (Cambridge, UK: Cambridge University Press).

16. Stadt Freiburg, "Bezahlbar Wohnen 2030 (Affordable Housing 2030)," 2020, https://www.freiburg.de/pb/site/Freiburg/get/params_E-318026111/1770796/Gesamtkonzept_Wohnen.pdf.

17. Stattbau GmbH and Netzwerkagentur Generationen-Wohnen, "Wohnen in Gemeinschaft Von der Idee zum gemeinsamen Haus (Living in a Community from the Idea to the Joint Home)," Stattbau, May 2015, https://www.stadtentwicklung.berlin.de/wohnen/wohnungsbau/download/wohnen_in_gemeinschaft.pdf.

18. Stadt Hamburg, "Unterstützung durch die Stadt Aufgaben der Agentur für Baugemeinschaften (Support from the City: Tasks of the Department for Building Communities)," accessed November 1, 2023, https://www.hamburg.de/baugemeinschaften/ansprechpartner-agentur-fuer-baugemeinschaften.

19. Organisation for Economic Co-operation and Development, "The Governance of Land Use in the Netherlands: The Case of Amsterdam Policy Highlights," 2017, https://www.oecd.org/regional/regionaldevelopment/Amsterdam-Policy-Highlights-EN.pdf.

20. Architectenweb, "Amsterdam investeert in groei aantal Wooncoöperaties (Amsterdam Invests in the Growth of the Number of Housing Cooperatives)," May 14, 2020, https://architectenweb.nl/nieuws/artikel.aspx?ID=47604.

Chapter 12

1. Whitney Airgood-Obrycki and Jennifer Molinsky, "Estimating the Gap in Affordable and Available Rental Units for Families," Joint Center for Housing Studies of Harvard University, April 2019, https://www.jchs.harvard.edu/sites/default/files/media/imp/harvard_jchs_family_sized_rental_housing_2019.pdf.

2. Stephanie H. Murray, "Cities Aren't Built for Kids," *The Atlantic*, July 7, 2022, https://www.theatlantic.com/family/archive/2022/07/raising-kid-american-city/661506/.

3. Brian McKenzie, "Transit Access and Population Change: The Demographic Profiles of Rail-Accessible Neighborhoods in the Washington, DC Area," US Census, Working paper no. SEHSD-WP2015-23, December 15, 2015, https://www.census.gov/library/working-papers/2015/demo/SEHSD-WP2015-23.html.

4. Zürcher Kantonalbank, "Kinder, wir bleiben in der Stadt (Children, We're Staying in the City)," April 2023, https://www.zkb.ch/de/blog/immobilien/kinder-wir-bleiben-in-der-stadt.html.

5. City of Vancouver, "High Density Housing for Families with Children Guidelines," amended July 20, 2022, https://guidelines.vancouver.ca/guidelines-high-density-housing-for-families-with-children.pdf.

6. Seattle Planning Commission, "Family-Sized Housing an Essential Ingredient to Attract and Retain Families with Children in Seattle," September 2014, https://www.seattle.gov/documents/Departments/SeattlePlanningCommission/AffordableHousingAgenda/FamSizePC_dig_final1.pdf.

7. San Francisco Planning Department, "Housing for Families with Children," January 17, 2017, https://default.sfplanning.org/publications_reports/Family_Friendly_Briefing_01-17-17_FINAL.pdf.

8. Stephen Smith, "Why We Can't Build Family-Sized Apartments in North America," Center for Building in North America, May 4, 2023, https://www.centerforbuilding.org/blog/we-we-cant-build-family-sized-apartments-in-north-america.

Chapter 13

1. Doug Gordon, "Not Just Bikes with Jason Slaughter," *The War on Cars* Podcast, Ep. 74, 4:00, November 30, 2021, https://thewaroncars.org/2021/11/30/not-just-bikes-with-jason-slaughter/.

2. Quoctrung Bui and Emily Badger, "The Coronavirus Quieted City Noise. Listen to What's Left." *The New York Times*, May 22, 2020, https://www.nytimes.com/interactive/2020/05/22/upshot/coronavirus-quiet-city-noise.html.

3. The Guardian Staff, "'Noise Radar' in Paris Will Catch Raucous Cars and Motorbikes," *The Guardian*, February 14, 2022, https://www.theguardian.com/world/2022/feb/15/noise-radar-in-paris-will-catch-raucous-cars-and-motorbikes.

4. Daniel Oleksiuk, "Confining Rental Homes to Busy Roads Is a Devil's Bargain," *The Tyee*, October 25, 2001, https://thetyee.ca/Analysis/2021/10/25/Confining-Rental-Homes-To-Busy-Roads-Devil-Bargain.

5. Benjamin Schneider, "New Law Represents 'Seismic Shift' in California Housing Policy," *San Francisco Examiner*, September 8, 2022, https://www.sfexaminer.com/our_sections/fixes/new-law-represents-seismic-shift-in-california-housing-policy/article_d3b78e5e-2ef6-11ed-9d55-933b202d19b2.html.

6. Mike Lindblom, "Seattle's Most Dangerous Light-Rail Stretch—and How to Make It Safer," *Seattle Times*, June 19, 2022, https://www.seattletimes.com/seattle-news/transportation/the-worst-spots-for-light-rail-crashes-in-seattle-and-how-to-fix-them.

7. Sara F. Camilleri et al., "All-Cause NO_2-Attributable Mortality Burden and Associated Racial and Ethnic Disparities in the United States," *Environmental Science & Technology Letters*, November 7, 2023, doi:10.1021/acs.estlett.3c00500.

8. Iona Cheng et al., "Traffic-Related Air Pollution and Lung Cancer Incidence: The California Multiethnic Cohort Study," *American Journal of Respiratory and Critical Care Medicine*, 2022, doi:10.1164/rccm.202107-1770OC.

9. Christopher G. Nolte et al., "Ch. 13: Air Quality," *Impacts, Risks, and Adaptation in the United States: Fourth National Climate Assessment*, volume II (Washington, DC: US Global Change Research Program, 2018), https://nca2018.globalchange.gov/chapter/13.

10. European Environment Agency, "Good Practice Guide on Noise Exposure and Potential Health Effects," Publications Office, 2010, https://data.europa.eu/doi/10.2800/54080.

11. Manuella Lech Cantuaria et al., "Residential Exposure to Transportation Noise in Denmark and Incidence of Dementia: National Cohort Study," *BMJ* (Clinical research ed.), September 8, 2021, doi:10.1136/bmj.n1954.

12. Environmental Protection Agency, "EPA History: Noise and the Noise Control Act," https://www.epa.gov/history/epa-history-noise-and-noise-control-act.

13. U.S. Congress, "House Resolution 4892—Quiet Communities Act of 2021," 2021, https://www.congress.gov/bill/117th-congress/house-bill/4892.

14. HUD, "24 CFR B—Noise Abatement and Control," April 1, 2013, https://www.govinfo.gov/app/details/CFR-2013-title24-vol1/CFR-2013-title24-vol1-part51-subpartB.

15. HUD, *HUD Noise Guidebook*, March 2009, https://www.hudexchange.info/programs/environmental-review/noise-abatement-and-control.

16. European Commission, "Environmental Noise Directive," July 29, 2021, https://environment.ec.europa.eu/topics/noise/environmental-noise-directive_en.

17. Peter Yeung, "Europe's Noise Capital Tries to Turn Down the Volume," Bloomberg, April 26, 2022, https://www.bloomberg.com/news/features/2022-04-27/how-paris-is-waging-a-war-on-noise-pollution.

18. Federal Republic of Germany, "Verkehrslärmschutzverordnung—16. BImSchV (Traffic Noise Protection Ordinance)," November 4, 2020, https://www.gesetze-im-internet.de/bimschv_16/index.html.

19. German Institute for Norms [DIN], "DIN 18005-1 Schallschutz im Staedtebau: Grundlagen und Hinweise für die Planung (Sound Insulation in Urban Planning: Fundamentals and Guidance for Planning)," July 2023, https://www.din.de/de/mitwirken/normenausschuesse/nabau/veroeffentlichungen/wdc-beuth:din21:363829655.

20. Meta Berghauser Pont, Jens Forssén, Marie Haeger-Eugensson, and Andreas Gustafson, "Increasing Cities' Capacity to Manage Noise and Air Quality Using Urban Morphology," *Book of Abstracts XXVI International Seminar on Urban Form, "Cities as Assemblages"* 42–42, July 6, 2019, https://research.chalmers.se/en/publication/514496.

21. Meta Berghauser Pont, Jens Forssén, Marie Haeger-Eugensson, Andreas Gustafson, and Niklas Rosholm, "Using Urban Form to Increase the Capacity of Cities to Manage Noise and Air Quality," *Urban Morphology* 27 (March 20, 2023): 51–69, doi:10.51347/UM27.0003.

22. Treberspurg & Partner Architekten, "Kaisermuehlenstrasse 22," https://www.treberspurg.com/projekt/passivhausanlage-kaisermuehlenstrasse.

Chapter 14

1. Nadja Kabisch, Matilda van den Bosch, and Raffaele Lafortezza, "The Health Benefits of Nature-Based Solutions to Urbanization Challenges for Children and the Elderly—A Systematic Review," *Environmental Research* 159 (2017): 362–373, doi:10.1016/j.envres.2017.08.004.

2. World Health Organization, "Urban Green Spaces and Health—a Review of Evidence," 2016.

3. Mathew P. White et al., "Would You Be Happier Living in a Greener Urban Area? A Fixed-Effects Analysis of Panel Data," *Psychological Science* 24, no. 6 (April 23, 2013): 920–928, doi:10.1177/0956797612464659.

4. Alessandro Rigolon, Matthew Browning, and Viniece Jennings, "Inequities in the Quality of Urban Park Systems: An Environmental Justice Investigation of Cities in the United States," *Landscape and Urban Planning* 178 (2018): 156–169, doi:10.1016/j.landurbplan.2018.05.026.

5. World Health Organization, "Urban Green Spaces: A Brief for Action," 2017, https://www.who.int/europe/publications/i/item/9789289052498.

6. Billie Giles-Corti et al., "Increasing Walking: How Important Is Distance to, Attractiveness, and Size of Public Open Space?," *American Journal of Preventive Medicine* 28, no. 2, suppl. 2 (2005) 169–176, doi:10.1016/j.amepre.2004.10.018.

7. Roland Sturm and Deborah Cohen, "Proximity to Urban Parks and Mental Health," *The Journal of Mental Health Policy and Economics* 17, no. 1 (2014): 19–24.

8. Lai Fern Ow and Subhadip Ghosh, "Urban Cities and Road Traffic Noise: Reduction through Vegetation," *Applied Acoustics* 120 (2017): 15–20, doi:10.1016/j.apacoust.2017.01.007.

9. Timothy Van Renterghem, "Towards Explaining the Positive Effect of Vegetation on the Perception of Environmental Noise," *Urban Forestry & Urban Greening* 40 (2019): 133–144, doi:10.1016/j.ufug.2018.03.007.

10. B. J. Park, Yuko Tsunetsugu, Tamami Kasetani, et al., "The Physiological Effects of Shinrin-yoku (Taking In the Forest Atmosphere or Forest Bathing): Evidence from Field Experiments in 24 Forests across Japan," *Environmental Health and Preventive Medicine* 15 (May 2, 2009): 18–26, doi:10.1007/s12199-009-0086-9.

11. Tegel Project GmbH, "Biodiversity: Building for People," https://schumacher-quartier.de/en/biodiversity/.

12. Studio Animal Aided Design, "Method: Including Wildlife into Urban Planning," https://animal-aided-design.de/en/method.

13. Kwan Ok Lee, Ke Michael Mai, and Souneil Park, "Green Space Accessibility Helps Buffer Declined Mental Health during the COVID-19 Pandemic: Evidence from Big Data in the United Kingdom," *Nature Mental Health* 1 (2023): 124–134, doi:10.1038/s44220-023-00018-y.

14. Roland Sturm and Deborah Cohen, "Suburban Sprawl and Physical and Mental Health," *Public Health* 118, no. 7 (2004): 488–496, doi:10.1016/j.puhe.2004.02.007.

15. European Commission, "Green City Accord: Clean and Healthy Cities for Europe," 2020, doi:10.2779/476324.

Chapter 15

1. Jessica Whitt and Scott Gordon, "This Is the Economic Cost of Extreme Weather," *World Economic Forum*, January 17, 2023, https://www.weforum.org/agenda/2023/01/extreme-weather-economic-cost-wef23.

2. Mariana Madruga de Brito and Mariele Evers, "Multi-Criteria Decision-Making for Flood Risk Management: A Survey of the Current State of the Art," *Natural Hazards and Earth System Sciences* 16 (April 26, 2016): 1019–1033, doi:10.5194/nhess-16-1019-2016.

3. World Bank, "What You Need to Know about Nature-Based Solutions to Climate Change," May 19, 2022, https://www.worldbank.org/en/news/feature/2022/05/19/what-you-need-to-know-about-nature-based-solutions-to-climate-change.

4. UN-Habitat, "Urbanization and Development: Emerging Futures. World Cities Report 2016," 2016, https://unhabitat.org/sites/default/files/download-manager-files/WCR-2016-WEB.pdf.

5. John Ruwitch, "Making Cities 'Spongy' Could Help Fight Flooding—by Steering the Water Underground," NPR, October 3, 2023, https://www.npr.org/2023/10/03/1202252103/china-floods-sponge-cities-climate-change.

6. Kuei-Hsien Liao, "A Theory on Urban Resilience to Floods—a Basis for Alternative Planning Practices," *Ecology and Society* 17, no. 4 (2012): 48, doi:10.5751/ES-05231-170448.

7. IBA Hamburg, "The Connected City Oberbillwerder Masterplan," City of Hamburg, January 2019, https://www.oberbillwerder-hamburg.de/wp-content/uploads/Master_Plan_Oberbillwerder_english_2019_web.pdf.

8. Mihir Zaveri, Matthew Haag, Adam Playford, and Nate Schweber, "How the Storm Turned Basement Apartments into Death Traps," *The New York Times*, September 2, 2021, https://www.nytimes.com/2021/09/02/nyregion/basement-apartment-floods-deaths.html.

9. Matt Simon, "If You Don't Already Live in a Sponge City, You Will Soon," *WIRED*, October 17, 2022, https://www.wired.com/story/if-you-dont-already-live-in-a-sponge-city-you-will-soon.

10. Saleh Shadman et al., "The Carbon Sequestration Potential of Urban Public Parks of Densely Populated Cities to

Improve Environmental Sustainability," *Sustainable Energy Technologies and Assessments* 52A (2022), doi:10.1016/j.seta.2022.102064.

11. US Environmental Protection Agency, "Reducing Urban Heat Islands: Compendium of Strategies. Draft," 2008, https://www.epa.gov/heat-islands/heat-island-compendium.

12. Mesfin M. Mekonnen and Arjen Y. Hoekstra, "Four Billion People Facing Severe Water Scarcity," *Science Advances* 2, no. 2 (February 12, 2016), https://www.science.org/doi/10.1126/sciadv.1500323.

13. Victoria Bisset, "Rich People's Swimming Pools Are Fueling Water Crises in Cities, Study Says," *The Washington Post*, April 11, 2023, https://www.washingtonpost.com/climate-environment/2023/04/11/water-crisis-swimming-pool-cape-town.

14. The Bullitt Center, "Composting Toilets: Lessons Learned," March 16, 2021, https://bullittcenter.org/2021/03/16/composting-toilets-lessons-learned.

15. AnEco, "The Aneco Association," https://an-eco.ch/aneco/.

Chapter 16

1. Wolfgang Feist, "The World's First Passive House, Darmstadt-Kranichstein, Germany," Passipedia, https://passipedia.org/examples/residential_buildings/multi-family_buildings/central_europe/the_world_s_first_passive_house_darmstadt-kranichstein_germany?s[]=kranichstein.

2. Wolfgang Feist et al., "25 Years of Passive House in Darmstadt Kranichstein," Passivhaus Institut, Darmstadt, 2016.

3. Ann Carrns, "How to Save on High Heating Bills This Winter," *The New York Times*, November 11, 2022, https://www.nytimes.com/2022/11/11/your-money/heating-bills-costs-winter.html.

4. The Passive House Network, "Safe at Home: How All-Electric, Multi-Family Passive House Buildings Deliver Comfortable, Cost-Effective Climate Resilience," https://passivehousenetwork.org/wp-content/uploads/2023/07/Passive-House-Network-Summer-2023-Report-Safe-at-Home.pdf.pdf.

5. Sharon Libby and Greta Tjeltveit, "Hobson Place: PH Supportive Housing in Seattle," Passive House Accelerator webinar, March 21, 2022, 31:35, https://youtu.be/9coWMaxjc_I.

6. US Department of Energy, "Air Sealing: Building Envelope Improvements," 2005, https://www.energystar.gov/ia/home_improvement/home_sealing/AirSealingFS_2005.pdf.

7. Patrick Sisson, "The Quest for the Smoke-Proof Building," Bloomberg, June 12, 2023, https://www.bloomberg.com/news/articles/2023-06-12/wildfire-smoke-draws-attention-to-indoor-air-quality-technology.

8. Chryssa Thousa and Jonathan Hines, "Post-Occupancy Evaluation of Five Schools by Architype," *Architects' Journal*, April 7, 2016, https://www.architectsjournal.co.uk/buildings/post-occupancy-evaluation-of-five-schools-by-architype.

9. Lenni Antonelli, "Passive Office Cuts Bills by £25k and Absenteeism by 13 Percent," Passive House Plus, October 30, 2015, https://passivehouseplus.ie/magazine/new-build/passive-office-cuts-bills-by-25k-and-absenteeism-by-13-percent.

10. Jing Zhao, "Passivhaus Standard as a Social Housing Model in the UK: Barriers and Opportunities," *SDGs in the European Region, Implementing the UN Sustainable Development Goals—Regional Perspectives*, ed. W. Leal Filho, M. A. P. Dinis, S. Moggi, E. Price, and A Hope (Cham, Switzerland: Springer, April 12, 2023), doi:10.1007/978-3-030-91261-1_87-1.

11. Sneha Ayyagari, Michael Gartman, and Jacob Corvidae, "Hours of Safety in Cold Weather," Rocky Mountain Institute, February 2020, https://rmi.org/wp-content/uploads/2020/02/Hours-of-Safety-insight-brief.pdf.

12. Massachusetts Department of Energy Resources, "2023 Technical Guidance: Massachusetts Stretch Energy Codes," 2023, https://www.mass.gov/doc/2023-stretch-code-technical-guidance-document-main-text/download.

13. Enrico Bonilauri, "Emu Report on Building Standards," November 27, 2023, https://passivehousenetwork.org/emu-report-energy-standards-california-results/.

14. US Green Building Council, "Minimum Energy Performance," https://www.usgbc.org/credits/retail-new-construction/v4/ea103.

15. EPBD, "Directive 2010/31/EU of the European Parliament and of the Council of 19 May 2010 on the Energy Performance of Buildings (Recast)," *Official Journal of the European Union*, 2010.

16. Mark Standen, Adam Tilford, and Kym Mead, "Be.Passive: Lessons Learnt from the Belgian Passivhaus Experience," Centre for the Built Environment, March 2013, https://www.passivhaustrust.org.uk/UserFiles/File/BePassive%20Report.pdf.

17. Jon Smijea, "A Natural Choice: The Challenges of Nature and LBC at Yellowstone National Park," *Trim Tab*, the International Living Future Institute, July 7 2020, https://trimtab.living-future.org/living-building-challenge/lbc-at-yellowstone-national-park/.

18. Patsy Healsy, "ILFI and Passive House Institute Announce New Crosswalk," *Trim Tab*, the International Living Future Institute, July 18, 2019, https://trimtab.living-fu

ture.org/blog/ilfi-and-passive-house-institute-announce-new-crosswalk/.

19. Søren Peper, "Monitoring of Passive House Buildings in Heidelberg-Bahnstadt," Passive House Institute, October, 2016, https://passiv.de/downloads/05_heidelberg_bahnstadt_monitoring_report_en.pdf.

20. Passive House Institute, "Component Database for Windows," https://database.passivehouse.com/en/components/list/window?

Chapter 17

1. United Nations Environment Program, "Impacts of Summer 2003 Heat Wave in Europe, 2004," https://www.unisdr.org/files/1145_ewheatwave.en.pdf.

2. Michael Egilson et al., "Extreme Heat and Human Mortality: A Review of Heat-Related Deaths in B.C. in Summer 2021," Report to the Chief Coroner of British Columbia, 2022, https://www2.gov.bc.ca/assets/gov/birth-adoption-death-marriage-and-divorce/deaths/coroners-service/death-review-panel/extreme_heat_death_review_panel_report.pdf.

3. Jason Vogel, Jeremy Hess, et al., "In the Hot Seat: Saving Lives from Extreme Heat in Washington State," report prepared by the University of Washington's Climate Impacts Group, UW's Center for Health and the Global Environment, the Washington State Department of Health, the Office of the Washington State Climatologist, and Gonzaga University's Center for Climate, Society & the Environment, 2023, https://cig.uw.edu/projects/in-the-hot-seat-saving-lives-from-extreme-heat-in-washington-state/.

4. Brad Plumer and Elena Shao, "Heat Records Fall around the Globe as Earth Warms, Fast," *New York Times*, July 6, 2023, https://www.nytimes.com/2023/07/06/climate/climate-change-record-heat.html.

5. The White House Historical Association, "Awnings on the White House," https://www.whitehousehistory.org/photos/awnings-on-the-white-house.

6. Robert Klara, *The Hidden White House* (New York: Thomas Dunne Books, October 22, 2013).

7. Emily Landes, "Nearly $10M Settlement for 'Cooked' SF Condo Owners," *The Real Deal*, July 28, 2021, https://therealdeal.com/new-york/2021/07/28/nearly-10m-settlement-for-cooked-sf-condo-owners.

8. Department of Energy, "Keeping the Lights On in Our Neighborhoods during Power Outages," December 8, 2023, https://www.energy.gov/gdo/articles/keeping-lights-our-neighborhoods-during-power-outages.

9. Brian Stone Jr. et al., "Compound Climate and Infrastructure Events: How Electrical Grid Failure Alters Heat Wave Risk," *Environmental Science & Technology*, May 18, 2021, doi:10.1021/acs.est.1c00024.

10. A. A. Williams et al., "Building Vulnerability in a Changing Climate: Indoor Temperature Exposures and Health Outcomes in Older Adults Living in Public Housing during an Extreme Heat Event in Cambridge, MA," *International Journal of Environmental Research and Public Health*, July 4, 2019, doi:10.3390/ijerph16132373.

11. Canton Basel City Council, "Urban Climate Concept—on Climate-Adapted Settlement Development in the Canton of Basel-Stadt," 2021, https://www.stadtklima.bs.ch/dam/jcr:a7604f45-848d-4e14-8bff-690197c483b7/BVD_Stadtklimakonzept_2-Auflage_WEB.pdf.

12. Michael Baechler et al., "Building America Best Practices Series: Volume 7.1: Guide to Determining Climate Regions by County," United States, 2010, doi:10.2172/1068658.

13. Paul W. Stackhouse Jr. et al., "An Assessment of Actual and Potential Building Climate Zone Change and Variability from the Last 30 Years through 2100 Using NASA's MERRA and CMIP5 Simulations," International Conference for Energy and Climate for the Energy Industry (ICEM 2015), 2015, https://ntrs.nasa.gov/api/citations/20160006535/downloads/20160006535.pdf.

14. Winston Choi-Schagrin, "After the Storm, the Mold: Warming Is Worsening Another Costly Disaster," *New York Times*, October 4, 2022, https://www.nytimes.com/2022/10/04/climate/hurricane-ian-mold-home-remediation.html.

15. Lucas Davis, Paul Gertler, Stephen Jarvis, and Catherine Wolfram, "Air Conditioning and Global Inequality," *Global Environmental Change*, July 2021, doi:10.1016/j.gloenvcha.2021.102299.

16. Francisco Salamanca et al., "Anthropogenic Heating of the Urban Environment Due to Air Conditioning," *Journal of Geophysical Research: Atmospheres*, 2014, doi:10.1002/2013jd021225.

17. Project Drawdown, "Refrigerant Management," https://drawdown.org/solutions/refrigerant-management.

18. Anna Kodé, "America, the Bland," *The New York Times*, January 20, 2023, https://www.nytimes.com/2023/01/20/realestate/housing-developments-city-architecture.html.

19. Jonas Schwaab et al., "The Role of Urban Trees in Reducing Land Surface Temperatures in European Cities," *Nature Communications*, December 2021, doi:10.1038/s41467-021-26768-w.

20. Alexandra Rempel et al., "Improving the Passive Survivability of Residential Buildings During Extreme Heat Events in the Pacific Northwest," *Applied Energy*, September 1, 2022, doi:10.1016/j.apenergy.2022.119323.

21. Building Design + Construction, "California Supreme Court Rules that Architects Can Be Sued by Condo

Association," 2015, https://www.bdcnetwork.com/california-supreme-court-rules-architects-can-be-sued-condo-association?page=209.

Chapter 18

1. Gerhard Schickhofer and Thomas Bogensperger, "Brettsperrholz," holz.bau forschungs gmbh, March 31, 2010, https://pure.tugraz.at/ws/portalfiles/portal/3335279/2010_03_31_Volnye_bogensperger_20100331.pdf.

2. https://www.woodworks.org/resources/mapping-mass-timber/.

3. WSP, "5 Thoughts on Mass Timber," January 4, 2022, https://www.wsp.com/en-gl/insights/5-thoughts-on-mass-timber.

4. Roxane Ward, "Going to New Heights," *Structure*, August 2009, 22.

5. Lydia Lee, "How Mass Timber Could Help Reduce Wildfire Risk," *Metropolis*, December 9, 2020, https://metropolismag.com/viewpoints/mass-timber-wildfire/.

6. "Structurlam Files for Bankruptcy Protection, Announces Sale," *Arkansas Democrat-Gazette*, April 24, 2023, https://www.arkansasonline.com/news/2023/apr/24/structurlam-files-for-bankruptcy-protection-announces-sale/.

7. Deimel Oelschlaeger Architekten, "Quartier Weissensee," https://www.deimeloelschlaeger.de/projekt/quartier-weissensee/.

8. Christoph Oelschlaeger, "Das Quartier WIR in Berlin-Weissensee," filmed December 2021 for BDA Bonn-Rhein-Sieg, video, 19:40, https://youtu.be/h_PBHuz9ez4.

9. Landeshauptstadt München, "Prinz-Eugen-Park," https://stadt.muenchen.de/infos/prinz-eugen-park.html.

10. ArchitekturWerkstattVallentin, "Baugemeinschaft Team[3]," https://www.vallentin-architektur.de/projekt/team-hoch-drei/.

11. Tegel Project GmbH, "Project Bauhütte 4.0—Cluster for Innovative Construction with Wood," https://schumacher-quartier.de/wp-content/uploads/2023/05/221123_Holzbau_EN.pdf.

12. Abhijeet Mishra et al., "Land Use Change and Carbon Emissions of a Transformation to Timber Cities," *Nature Communications* 13 (August 30, 2022): 4889, doi:10.1038/s41467-022-32244-w.

13. Yanine Quiroz, "Halving Reliance on Meat and Dairy Could Cut Land-Use Emissions 'by 31%,'" *Carbon Brief*, September 12, 2023, https://www.carbonbrief.org/halving-reliance-on-meat-and-dairy-could-could-cut-land-use-emissions-by-31.

14. US Forest Service, "Wood Innovation," https://www.fs.usda.gov/science-technology/energy-forest-products/wood-innovation.

15. TMF, "The Proportion of Multi-Apartment Buildings with Wooden Frames Remains the Same," November 25, 2021, https://www.tmf.se/om-tmf/nyheter/2021/11/andelen-flerbostadshus-med-trastomme-haller-i-sig.

16. Bauen mit Holz, "Holzbau entwickelt sich gut (Wood Construction Is Developing Well)," October 27, 2023, https://www.bauenmitholz.de/holzbau-entwickelt-sich-gut-27102023.

17. Merel Pit, Catja Edens, and Igor Sladoljev, "Lessons in Circularity," *Cie*, September 10, 2021, p. 20.

18. City of Vienna, "Innovative Office Building Block System," December 12, 2017, https://smartcity.wien.gv.at/en/temporary-office-buildings-at-heldenplatz.

19. Matthias Heinrich and Werner Lang, "Materials Passports: Best Practices," Technische Universität München, in association with BAMB, February 2019, https://www.bamb2020.eu/wp-content/uploads/2019/02/BAMB_MaterialsPassports_BestPractice.pdf.

Chapter 19

1. United Nations Environment Programme and Yale Center for Ecosystems + Architecture, "Building Materials and the Climate: Constructing a New Future," Knowledge Repository, UNEP, 2023, https://wedocs.unep.org/20.500.11822/43293.

2. Katherina Simonen et al., "Life Cycle Assessment of Buildings: A Practice Guide," The Carbon Leadership Forum, June 2019, https://carbonleadershipforum.org/wp-content/uploads/2019/05/CLF-LCA-Practice-Guide_2019-05-23.pdf.

3. California Legislative Information, "AB-43 Greenhouse Gas Emissions: Building Materials: Embodied Carbon Trading System," October 7, 2023, https://leginfo.legislature.ca.gov/faces/billStatusClient.xhtml?bill_id=202320240AB43.

4. Danish Ministry of the Interior and Housing, "National Strategy for Sustainable Construction," April 2021, https://im.dk/Media/637602217765946554/National_Strategy_for_Sustainable_Construktion.pdf.

5. Bund Deutscher Architektinnen und Architekten (Association of German Architects), "Abrissmoratorium: Ein offener Brief (Demolition Moratorium, an Open Letter), September 19, 2022, https://www.bda-bund.de/2022/09/abrissmoratorium/.

6. Jorina Stuber, "Aus Blautalcenter wird Blau.Quartier: 1.000 Wohnungen geplant (Blautalcenter Becomes Blau.Quartier: 1,000 Homes Planned)," Südwestrundfunk, October 27, 2023, https://www.swr.de/swraktuell/baden-wuerttemberg/ulm/plaene-fuer-blautalcenter-ulm-100.html.

7. Jan Mischke et al., "Empty Spaces and Hybrid Places: The

Pandemic's Lasting Impact on Real Estate," McKinsey, July 13, 2023, https://www.mckinsey.com/mgi/our-research/empty-spaces-and-hybrid-places.

8. "Innovations," Erden, https://www.erden.at/Innovations.

9. haas cook zemmrich STUDIO2050, "Rammed Earth House Heilbronn," https://www.haascookzemmrich.com/en/projekte/rammed-earth-residential-house-heilbronn/.

10. Building Centre, "Stone Tower Research Project," March 25, 2020, https://www.buildingcentre.co.uk/news/articles/stone-tower-research-project.

11. Timothée de Toldi and Tristan Pestre, "The Relevance of Cut-Stone to Strategies for Low-Carbon Buildings," *Buildings and Cities* 4, no. 1): 229–257, doi:10.5334/bc.278.

12. Leah D. Ellis et al., "Toward Electrochemical Synthesis of Cement—An Electrolyzer-Based Process for Decarbonating $CaCO_3$ While Producing Useful Gas Streams," *Proceedings of the National Academy of Sciences* 117, no. 23 (September 16, 2019): 12584–12591, https://doi.org/10.1073/pnas.1821673116.

13. X-Fix, "X-fix C Type," accessed December 13, 2023, https://www.x-fix.at/x-fix-c-type.

14. EcoCocon, "Cradle to Cradle—Remaking the Way We Build," February 28, 2020, https://ecococon.eu/us/blog/2020/cradle-to-cradle-ecococon.

15. Hal Bernton, "A Giant Oregon Wildfire Shows the Limits of Carbon Offsets in Fighting Climate Change," Oregon Public Broadcasting, August 2, 2023, https://www.opb.org/article/2023/08/02/climate-change-carbon-offset-oregon/.

16. Lilli Kaarakka, Julia Rothey, and Laura E. Dee, "Managing Forests for Carbon—Status of the Forest Carbon Offset Markets in the United States," *PLoS Climate* 2, no. 7: e0000158, https://doi.org/10.1371/journal.pclm.0000158.

17. Querbeet GbR, "Das Project (the Project)," https://querbeet-lueneburg.de/das-projekt/.

Chapter 20

1. Sydney Lake, "Goldman Says Office Buildings Need a 50% Price Drop for Residential Conversion to Be a Real Thing," *Fortune*, February 28, 2024, https://fortune.com/2024/02/28/goldman-sachs-office-residential-conversions-price-cut.

2. American Institute of Architects, "Buildings That Last: Design for Adaptability, Deconstruction, and Reuse," December 4, 2023, https://content.aia.org/sites/default/files/2020-03/ADR-Guide-final_0.pdf.

3. N. John Habraken, *Supports: An Alternative to Mass Housing* (New York: Praeger, 1972): 59–60.

4. Sonja Lüthi and Marc Schwarz, "'DE DRAGER': A Film about Architect John Habraken," Schwarzpictures, Switzerland, January 13, 2013, https://vimeo.com/showcase/dedrager.

5. Open Building NL, "Case Studies," https://www.openbuilding.co/casestudies.

6. Patch 22, "Sustainability: Flexible Installations," http://patch22.nl/sustainability/#flexible-installation.

7. World Bank, "Converting Disaster Experience into a Safer Built Environment: The Case of Japan," May 2018, doi:10.1596/30015.

8. Kazuaki Nagata, "Japan's Scrap-and-Rebuild Culture Faces an Environmental Reckoning," *The Japan Times*, August 27, 2023, https://www.japantimes.co.jp/environment/2023/08/27/sustainability/japan-scrap-build-sustainability/.

9. Enlai Hooi, "Enlai Hooi—Schmidt Hammer Lassen Architects—Rocket and Tigerli—100 Meter Mass Timber Building" Oregon Mass Timber Network by Greg Howes, 1:55, https://youtu.be/DuO04sqjdOQ?si=EBZWrhTZWj71pm4i.

Epilogue

1. Conor Dougherty, "The Capital of Sprawl Gets a Radically Car-Free Neighborhood," *The New York Times,* October 31, 2020, https://www.nytimes.com/2020/10/31/business/culdesac-tempe-phoenix-sprawl.html.

2. Jordyn Pair, "Solar-Powered Community in Ann Arbor Opening Home Reservations on Earth Day," Mlive Media Group, April 21, 2022, https://www.mlive.com/news/ann-arbor/2022/04/solar-powered-community-in-ann-arbor-opening-home-reservations-on-earth-day.html.

3. Katie Barr, "Farm Stops: A New Way to Enhance Local and Regional Food Systems," *Resilience*, July 29, 2022, https://www.resilience.org/stories/2022-07-29/farm-stops-a-new-way-to-enhance-local-and-regional-food-systems.

4. Jennifer Van Grover, "Development Team Wants to Build 5,000 Apartments on San Diego's Sports Arena Site—With or Without an Arena," *San Diego Union Tribune*, December 14, 2021, https://www.sandiegouniontribune.com/business/growth-development/story/2021-12-14/development-team-wants-to-build-5-000-apartments-on-san-diegos-sports-arena-site-with-or-without-an-arena.

5. Northcrest Developments & Canada Lands Company, "Proposed Redevelopment of the Downsview Lands Framework Plan," September 2021, https://www.id8downsview.ca/progress.

6. Jan Gehl, *Cities for People* (Washington, DC: Island Press, 2010).

7. Rob Hopkins, *The Transition Handbook: From Oil Dependency to Local Resilience* (New York: Bloomsbury Publishing, 2008).

About the Author

Michael Eliason is a licensed architect and founder of Larch Lab—part architecture and urbanism studio, part "think and do" tank focusing on research and policy, decarbonized low-energy buildings, and climate adaptive urbanism. Michael is also a writer and an award-winning architect specializing in mass timber, social housing, Baugruppen (urban cohousing), and ecodistricts. His career has been dedicated to advancing innovation and broadening the discourse on sustainable development, Passive House, nonmarket housing, and decarbonized construction. He has helped usher several legislative efforts on point access blocks across the United States and is a founding board member of Seattle's Passive House Social Housing Developer Public Development Authority. Michael is a graduate of Virginia Tech and became a Certified Passive House Designer in 2010. His professional experience includes work in both the United States and Germany. He lives in Seattle with his wife and two children. They have been car-light and car-free for over a decade, having collected an assortment of bikes and cargo bikes to easily get around in an autocentric city while living their values.